MARRIAGE NOTICES

IN

Charleston Courier

1803-1808

Compiled and Edited by A. S. SALLEY, Jr.,
Secretary of the Historical Commission of South Carolina

From the files in the library of the Charleston Library Society,
Charleston, S. C.

GENEALOGICAL PUBLISHING CO., INC.
BALTIMORE 1976

Originally Published
Columbia, South Carolina
1919

Reprinted
Genealogical Publishing Co., Inc.
Baltimore, 1976

Library of Congress Catalogue Card Number 76-16889
International Standard Book Number 0-8063-0727-7

Made in the United States of America

INTRODUCTION

The first issue of a new paper, entitled *Charleston Courier*, appeared in Charleston, S. C., Monday morning, January 10, 1803. The business line just under the title head showed that it was "published (daily) by A. S. Willington, for Loring Andrews, at No. 6, Crafts's South Range" (now Adger's South Wharf) "At $7 per annum, payable in advance." Loring Andrews, its founder, was a young New Englander, a native of Hingham, Massachusetts. It had been his intention to issue his first paper on the first day of the year, but the vessel upon which his printing press was to arrive made an unusually long passage. Willington, like Andrews, was a New Englander, and a native of Massachusetts. He came to Charleston at the solicitation of Andrews to superintend the mechanical execution of his paper. His connection with the *Courier* ceased only with his death fifty-nine years later.

The *Charleston Courier* contained four pages, twenty by twelve inches in size, four columns to the page and was "delivered to Subscribers in the City, at their places of residence, and regularly transmitted by the Mails to those in the Country." The paper, type, dress and typography were all in the best style of the day. The first issue contained a "Prospectus" (taking up the first column) in which the editor discussed the importance and responsibilities of public journals; outlined his political policy, declaring himself a Federalist; declared it his intention to give the best news service, and to "provide articles of information and amusement for every description of readers", and furnished the conditions upon which the paper would be published, as given above. Then followed an account of the proceedings of Congress; a comparison between the monarchical and the consular despotisms of France (abridged from a London paper); British domestic intelligence; affairs in France; nearly two columns of editorial; "European Politics", news letters from New York and Boston; a clipping from *The Times;* a poem; "Marine Intelligence", and over a page of advertisements, including one of the Santee Canal Company. Associated with Andrews was Stephen Cullen Carpenter.

The next year Andrews secured some official patronage, for with the issue for Friday, November 30, 1804, the single business line that had been running just under the heading of the first page was so changed as to show Loring Andrews "Printer to the City." With the issue for Wednesday, July 10, 1805, this business line was further changed by substituting "the proprietor" for "Loring Andrews."

Andrews's proprietorship in the *Courier* was of short duration. In the issue for July 11, 1805, he announced that he had disposed of his interest in the *Charleston Courier*, and forthwith delivered his valedictory as a proprietor.

The issue for Monday, September 2, 1805, contained this announcement:

> The public is respectfully informed, that Mr. Loring Andrews's share in *The Courier* has been transferred to the Subscriber, and that he will be thankful for its patronage and support.
>
> Benjamin Burgh Smith.
>
> *The Courier* will hereafter be published under the firm of Benjamin Burgh Smith & Co.

Stephen Cullen Carpenter was the "Co." A. S. Willington's name ceased on that day to appear as publisher "for the proprietor", but he was still connected with its management. With the same issue the type of the title heading was changed from the plain block type theretofore used to Old English type.

Andrews was preparing to return to his home in the North when he was taken sick and died October 19, 1805. The *Courier* of the 21st contained an editorial on his death.

The issue for Friday, January 10, 1806, announced that Benjamin B. Smith had withdrawn from the *Courier* establishment and that the paper would in future be edited by Messrs. Carpenter, Dalcho, Marchant and Willington under the firm name of Marchant, Willington & Co. "The wreath or the rod" was adopted as the paper's motto and was placed immediately under the sub-title on the second page.

Smith was a native South Carolinian. His father was Roger Smith, descended from the first governor, James Moore, his son Roger Moore, Col. William Rhett, Col. Thomas Smith, Landgrave Thomas Smith, Barnard Schenckingh and others distinguished in the history of South Carolina, and his mother was Mary Rutledge, a sister of the great "Dictator" John Rutledge, President of South Carolina, Governor of South Carolina and sometime Chief-Justice of the Supreme Court of the United States. He was a lawyer by profession, having been admitted to the Bar in Charleston in 1797, and a Federalist in politics. A biographer says that he was remarkable for his wit as well as for his talent; distinguished for a courteous method of expression, and always showed a proper respect for the opinions of others.[1]

With the issue for Wednesday, November 18, 1807, Marchant, Willington & Co. insert "Printers to the City" in their announcement.

On December 1, 1807, the office of the *Courier* was removed from No. 1. to No. 143 Broad Street.

Carpenter, former partner of Messrs. Andrews and Smith and a member of the new firm, was an Irishman, well known as having been, at one time, a writer for the periodical press of London, reporter of the parliamentary proceedings during the trial consequent upon the impeachment of Warren Hastings by the British Government in 1788, and author of the *Overland Journey to India* under the pseudonym of Donald Campbell. He came to Charleston about the time that Andrews came and had intended establishing a paper, but seeing that two new papers could not succeed at that time, joined forces with Andrews. We find him, on July 30, 1804, issuing in the *Courier* a prospectus for a magazine to be called *The Monthly Register and Review of the United States.* This prospectus ran almost daily for several months. In the paper for August 4, 1804, he issued a statement as to his magazine that indicates that it was issued at the "office" of the *Courier.* King says that Carpenter withdrew from the firm of Marchant, Willington & Co. July 9, 1806,[2] but there is nothing in the columns of the *Courier* to confirm his statement. Just about that time Carpenter was calling for proposals for publishing his works and on July 19, there is a three column signed communication in the *Courier* from him anent some criticisms he had made of the performance of W. F. Youngschool (Dr. William Ioor): *The Battle of the Eutaw Springs*, and in an advertisement in the same paper he announced that he would sail for New York in a few days and called upon subscribers to his magazine to pay up.

With the issue for January 1, 1808, the *Charleston Courier* dropped the little business notice from the first column and added a sub-title which was used, however, only on the second page. It was there called *The Courier and Mercantile Daily Advertiser*, but this addition was dropped after the issue for December 5, 1808.

---

[1]King: *The Newspaper Press of Charleston* (1872), p. 96. [2]Ibid, p. 98.

Married.

In this city, on Thursday morning last, by the Rev. Dr. Buist, John Sanders, Esq. to Miss Eliza O'Hear, daughter of Mr. James O'Hear.

By the Rev. Mr. Azuby, Mr. Abraham Sasportas, merchant, to Miss Charlotte Canter.

By the Rev. Dr. Keith, capt. Francis Stiles Lightbourn, of this city, to Mrs. Eliza B. Edings, of Wadmalaw. (Friday, January 14, 1803.)

Married.

On Sunday evening last, by the Rev. Doctor Gallaher, Mr. James Guy, to Mrs. Grace Ingram, both of this city.

On Tuesday evening, Mr. Christian M. Logan, to Miss Sarah White Chanler, youngest daughter of the late Doctor Isaac Chanler. (Thursday, January 27, 1803.)

Married.

In this city, on Thursday evening last, by the Rev. Mr. Frost, Nathaniel Broughton Mazyck, Esquire, to Miss Christiana Boston Harris, third daughter of Doctor Tucker Harris.

In Greenville District, on Sunday the 16th inst, Mr. William Toney, to Mrs. Jane Benson, relict of Major Joseph Benson, deceased. (Saturday, January 29, 1803.)

Married.

On Thursday, the 20th ult. Mr. George Veree, merchant, of this city, to Miss Harriet Jarman, of St. James', Santee. (Wednesday, February 2, 1803.)

Married.

On Thursday evening last, by the Rev. Dr. Frost, Mr. Paul Pritchard, jun. to Miss Catharine Hamilton, both of this city.

On the 20th of December last, by the Rev. Dr. Buist, James Scott, Esq. planter, St. Andrew's parish, to the amiable and accomplished Miss Elizabeth Davis, of the same place. (Monday, February 14, 1803.)

MARRIED.

On Sunday last, Mr. George Medowes, to Miss Ann Margaret Attiner, both of this city.
On Tuesday evening last, by the Rev. Mr. Bowen, Dr. Foissin, to Miss Fayssoux, eldest daughter of the late Dr. Peter Fayssoux.
On Wednesday evening, Mr. Christopher Wagoner, to the amiable Mrs. Mary Critesburg. (Saturday, February 19, 1803.)

MARRIED,

On Wednesday evening last, by the Rev. Mr. Jenkins, Doctor Samuel Thomas, of Georgetown, to Miss Mary Gaillard, daughter of the late John Gaillard, Esq. (Monday, February 21, 1803.)

MARRIED,

On Sunday evening last, Mr. Robert Paterson, to the amiable Miss Ann Hampton—both of this city. (Wednesday, February 23, 1803.)

MARRIED,

On Tuesday evening last, by the Rev. Mr. Jenkins, William Lee, jun. Esq. Attorney at Law, to Miss Elizabeth Markley, daughter of Mr. Abraham Markley, merchant, of this city. (Thursday, February 24, 1803.)

MARRIED,

On the 9th inst. by the Rev. Dr. M'Calla, Mr. James Dorrill, of Christ Church Parish, to Miss Ann Dorrill of the same place.
On Tuesday evening last, by the Rev. Dr. Hollingshead, Mr. John Lequeux, factor, to Miss Martha Darrell, second daughter of Edward Darrell, Esq. merchant, deceased. (Friday, February 25, 1803.)

MARRIED,

At Augusta, on the 3d instant, Mr. John S. Adams, merchant of this city, to Miss Sarah Eve, daughter of Capt. Oswald Eve, of Augusta.
On Saturday evening last, by the Rev. Mr. Frost, Mr. Archibald Smith, jun. to Mrs. Ann Chevers, widow of the late Mr. Richard Holmes Chevers, both of this city. (Saturday, March 19, 1803.)

MARRIED.

On Thursday evening last, Mr. Joseph Hugoins, to Miss Ann Huger, daughter of Gen. Huger, both of Prince George's, Santee.[1] (Tuesday, March 22, 1803.)

MARRIED,

At his plantation in St. Andrews Parish, by the Rev. Mr. Mills, Doctor Joseph Chonler to Mrs. Mary Brune, widow of the late D. I. Brune, Esq. of New-York. (Tuesday, June 21, 1803.)

MARRIED,

On Saturday last, by the Rev. Dr. Thomas Frost, Mr. Joseph Assalit, late Planter of St. Domingo, to the accomplished Miss Magdalen Gosselin, of Bordeaux. (Wednesday, July 13, 1803.)

MARRIED,

At Acton, near Boston, Mr. Luke Bixly, of Boston, to Miss Nabby Adams. (Wednesday, August 10, 1803.)

MARRIED,

At Columbia, on the 8th ult. Mr. Nathaniel G. Welch, of this city, to the amiable and accomplished Miss Elizabeth Todd, of Columbia. (Tuesday, October 4, 1803.)

MARRIED,

On Sunday evening, by the Rev. Mr. Darley, Mr. John Furchase, to the amiable Miss Elizabeth Smith, both of this city.

On the 9th inst. by the Rev. Mr. Brazier, capt. Joseph Vesey, to the amiable Mrs. Blair, both of this city. (Tuesday, October 11, 1803.)

MARRIED,

On Tuesday Evening, by the Rev. Dr. Jenkins, Thomas Simons, Esq. to Miss Ann Simons, only daughter of Keating Simons, Esq. (Friday, October 28, 1803.)

MARRIED,

At Boston, by the Rev. Dr. Stillman, Mr. Normand McLeod, of South-Carolina, to Mrs. Elizabeth Vinson, of the former place. (Monday, November 7, 1803.)

[1]Prince George's Parish, Winyah, is correct.

MARRIED,

On the 8th inst. by the Rev. Mr. Faber, Mr. Christian Henry Faber, to Miss Catharine Lindauer, both of this city.
At Providence, R. I. Mr. David Chalmers, of this city, to Mrs. Margaretta Pinkerton, widow of David Pinkerton, merchant; of Philadelphia. (Thursday, November 10, 1803.)

MARRIED,

On Tuesday evening last, by the Rev. Dr. Frost, William Cattell, Esq. to Miss Mary Ladson, daughter of Major Ladson. (Friday, November 11, 1803.)

MARRIED,

On Thursday evening last, by the Rev. John Thompson, Mr. Alexander Doke, to Mrs. Deborah Willingham, both of this city. (Tuesday, November 22, 1803.)

MARRIED,

At Savannah, on Thursday, the 1st inst. by the Rev. Mr. Clarkson, Mr. George H. Davidson, merchant, to Miss Sarah C. Bellinger, eldest daughter of B. B. Bellinger, Esq. of South-Carolina. (Wednesday, December 7, 1803.)

MARRIED,

On Thursday evening last, by the Rev. Dr. Hollingshead, Mr. William Zuill, of Blackmingo, to the amiable and agreeable Miss Mary Ann McClusken, of this city. (Wednesday, December 21, 1803.)

Married, on Wednesday, the 22d instant, by the Rev. Dr. Hollingshead, Mr. Lawrence Benson to Mrs. Mary Ingraham, both of this city. (Wednesday, December 28, 1803.)

Married, on Wednesday evening, the 14th inst. in Georgetown, Isaac Minis, Esq. of Savannah, to Miss Cohen, eldest daughter of Solomon Cohen, Esq. of the former place. (Friday, December 30, 1803.)

Married, on the 31st ultimo, by the Rev. George Buist, Mr. Rupert Kirk, to the amiable Miss Jane Nubey, lately from New-York. (Monday, January 2, 1804.)

Married, on Sunday last, by the Rev. Mr. Frost, Mr. John Simpson, merchant, to Miss Mary Godfrey, only daughter of Mr. Thomas Godfrey of this city. (Thursday, January 5, 1804.)

Married, in Baltimore, on Saturday, the 24th ult. Jerome Bonaparte to Miss Elizabeth Patterson, eldest daughter of Mr. William Patterson, merchant of that city. (Wednesday, January 11, 1804.)

Married, on Tuesday evening last, by the Rev. Dr. Keith, Mr. Bethel Threadcraft, to Miss Sarah Yates, both of this city. (Thursday, January 19, 1804.)

Married, at Athens, (Vermont) Master Silas Chaplin, aged fifteen, to Miss Susannah Powers, aged thirteen!!

Little Jack Horner, sat in the corner,
Eating a piece Christmas pie,
He put in his thumb, and pull'd out a plumb,
Crying what a brave boy am I!!

(Monday, January 30, 1804.)

Married, by the Rev. T. D. Bladen, at Ashepoo, on the 1st instant, Francis Fishburn, Esq. to Miss Mary C. Bellenger, the youngest daughter of the late Edmund Bellenger, Esq. (Tuesday, February 7, 1804.)

Married, last Tuesday evening, by the Rev. Dr. Buist, Mr. David Haig to Miss Maria Annely, both of this city. (Thursday, March 1, 1804.)

Married, on Wednesday evening last, by the Rev. Mr. Fraser, Mr. Samuel Campbell, of Baltimore, to Miss Ann Buford, of this city. (Saturday, March 3, 1804.)

Married,

At the High Hills of Santee, on Thursday evening last, by the Rev. John M. Roberts, Mr. Merry Bracey to Miss Elcey Moore, both of that place.

On Thursday evening last, by the Rev. Mr. Bowen, Daniel Huger, Esq. to Miss Sarah L. Lance, daughter of Colonel Lambert Lance, both of this city. (Wednesday, March 7, 1804.)

MARRIED, on Thursday evening, by the Rev. Dr. Isaac S. Keith, Benjamin Stiles, junr. Esq. of Wadmalaw Island, to Miss Rebecca Theus, eldest daughter of Major Simeon Theus, of this city.
—on Thursday the 29th of March last, by the Rev. Mr. Knox, Mr. Samuel R. Mouzon of Black Mingo, to the amiable Miss Mary Simons, near that place.
—on the 10th instant, by the Rev. Mr. Botsford, John Presley, Esq. of Black Mingo, to the amiable and accomplished Miss Mary Brockington, daughter of the late Capt. John Brockington, all of that place. (Saturday, April 14, 1804.)

Married, on Sunday evening, by the Rev. Mr. Munds, Mr. John Speissegger, of this place, to Miss Wilhelmina Christiana Heinrichs, of Delmenhorst near Bremen. (Tuesday, April 17, 1804.)

Married, on Thursday evening, 26th inst. by the Reverend J. Munds, Mr. Thomas Fitzgerald Quin to Mrs. Eliza Lesesne, both of this city.
—same evening by the Rev. Mr. Munds, Mr. David Ross, to Miss Susannah Fowler Robinson, both of this place.
—same evening, by the Rev. Mr. Munds, Mr. Laben Slade, to Mrs. Mary Ann Coalfoard, both of this place.
—same evening, by the Rev. Dr. Furman, Mr. John G. Stevenson, of this city, to Miss Lucinda Christian, of Georgetown, S. C.
—on Saturday evening last, by the Rev. Mr. Malcomson, Mr. Robert Gordon, merchant of Philadelphia, to Miss Nancy Fleming, of this city. (Saturday, April 28, 1804.)

Married, on Monday evening, by the Rev. Dr. Frost, Mr. John Query, to Miss Honoria Mills, second daughter of the reverend Dr. Mills. (Wednesday, May 9, 1804.)

Married, on Sunday last, 27th inst. by the Rev. Solomon Hart, Mr. Solomon Levy, merchant, to Mrs. Hannah Levy, relict of the late Samuel Levy, both of this city. (Tuesday, May 29, 1804.)

Married, on Thursday evening, by the Rev. Mr. Malcomson, Mr. William Simms, merchant, to Miss Harriet Singleton, both of this city.[1] (Saturday, June 2, 1804.)

[1]The parents of William Gilmore Simms (1806-1870), the writer.

Married, the 5th instant, by the Rev. John Thompson, in St. Philip's Parish, Mr. John Withers, jun. to Miss Mary Bowen, only daughter of John Bowen, Esq. of Goose Creek, Planter. (Thursday, June 7, 1804.)

Married, on Thursday evening last, at Givhan's Ferry, by the Rev. Mr. Palmer, Mr. James Maull, merchant, of Jacksonborough, to the amiable Miss Mary Givhan, youngest daughter of Philip Givhan, Esq.
—, at Rumney, on the 17th inst. by the Rev. Dr. Keith, Henry Kennon, Esq, to Mrs. Rebecca Mege, relict of Francis Mege, Esq. formerly of St. Domingo.
—, on Monday evening, by the Rev. Dr. Hollingshead, Rev. Dr. Isaac S. Keith, to Miss Jane Huxham. (Wednesday, June 20, 1804.)

Married, on the 23d last Month, Captain Thomas Campbell Cox, one of the Editors of "*The Times*," to Miss Susan Mason Skrine. (Wednesday, July 11, 1804.)

Married, on Tuesday evening last, by the Rev. Dr. Hollingshead, Mr. Sears Hubble to Miss Charlotte Henrietta Broeskie, both of this city. (Friday, July 13, 1804.)

Married, on Tuesday evening last, the 17th inst. by the Rev. Mr. Malcomson, Mr. Moses Sandford, to Miss Margaret Welch. (Monday, July 23, 1804.)

Married, on Saturday evening last, by the Rev. Mr. Hollingshead, Mr. Joseph Lesesne, of Georgetown, to Miss Ann Fowler, of this city. (Tuesday, July 31, 1804.)

Married, on Thursday evening last, by the Rev. Mr. Munds, Mr. Wm. W. Norton, of Rhode-Island, to Miss Mary Salter, of this city, late of Philadelphia. (Saturday, August 4, 1804.)

Married—On Tuesday evening last, by the Rev. Mr. Kenrick, Mr. Isaac Weatherly, to the amiable Miss Rachel Rambert, both of this city. (Saturday, August 18, 1804.)

Married, on the 2d inst. in Laurens County, by the Rev. Dr. Kennedy, John Bowen, Esq. of Goose-creek, planter, to Miss Rebecca Withers, daughter of John Withers, Esq. of Laurens County.[1] (Wednesday, August 29, 1804.)

Married—in England, the 12th of June last, the Earl of Moria,[2] to the Countess of Loudon. (Monday, September 3, 1804.)

Married, on Tuesday evening, by the Rev. Dr. Keith, Doctor Joseph Glover, to Miss Eliza Yonge. (Friday, September 14, 1804.)

Married, on Saturday evening last, by the Rev. Dr. Furman, Mr. James Tomlins, to Miss Letitia Cape, both of this city. (Thursday, September 20, 1804.)

Married, on Thursday evening, Mr. Henry Barnstine, to Mrs. C. Wyant, both of this city.
Married, on Thursday evening, by the Rev. Mr. Mills, Mr. Daniel Boyden, to Miss Mary Henry, both of this city.
Married, at New-York, on the 18th ult, by the Rev. Dr. Roe, Mr. Thomas Tait, of this city, to Miss Elizabeth Noble, of the former place. (Saturday, October 6, 1804.)

Married, on Saturday, the 13th inst. by the Rev. Dr. Munds, Mr. John Gray Green, to Mrs. Mary Susannah Austin, both of this city.
Married, on Thursday last, Mr. Thomas Lesesne to Miss Ann Broun; both of this city.
Married, on the 20th ult. by Charles Griffin, esq. Mr. Isaac Waldrop, to the amiable Miss Jenny Davidson; both of Newberry district. (Tuesday, October 16, 1804.)

Married, on Wednesday evening, by the Rev. Dr. Keith, Thomas Ogier, Esq. merchant, to Miss Sarah Henley. (Friday, November 2, 1804.)

---

[1]District, not County.

[2]This was Lord Rawdon of detestable memory in South Carolina. The Countess of Loudoun was Flora Muir (Campbell).

Married on Thursday evening, at St. Andrew's parish, by the Rev. Dr. Price, Mr. John Thomas Smart, of this city, to Miss Mary Allston Rivers, of said parish, youngest daughter of Joseph Rivers, esq. planter, deceased.
Married on Thursday evening last, by the Rev. Dr. Hollingshead, Mr. Jacint Laval, jun. eldest son of Jacint Laval, esq. to Miss Frances Susanna Rivers, both of this place.
Married on Thursday evening last, by the Rev. Mr. Bowen, Mr. George Philippi Bechem, merchant, of Leghorn, to Miss Sarah Bradford, of this place. (Saturday, November 3, 1804.)

Married, on Saturday evening last, Mr. Simeon Bevens, to Miss Elizabeth Folker, both of this city.
Married, on Tuesday evening, by the Rev. Dr. Jenkins, Mr. N. Bixby, merchant, to Miss Foissin, both of this city. (Thursday, November 15, 1804.)

Married, on Wednesday evening last, by the Rev. Dr. Hollingshead, Mr. George K. White, to Miss Rebecca Chambers, both of this city. (Saturday, November 17, 1804.)

Married, on Tuesday evening last, by the Rev. Dr. Jenkins, Mr. George Jouve, Planter, to Miss Susannah D. Schutt, daughter of the late Caspar C. Schutt, Esqr. of this city, merchant. (Monday, November 19, 1804.)

Married, on Monday evening last, at Toogado, Mr. James Swinton, factor, to Miss Eliza Bailey. (Wednesday, November 21, 1804.)

Married, on Tuesday evening the 20th inst. by the Rev. Dr. Wm. Holſingshead, John Mikell, Esq. planter, of Edisto Island, to Miss Sarah D. Wilkinson, eldest daughter of Capt. Joseph Wilkinson, of the state of Georgia, planter. (Thursday, November 29, 1804.)

Married, on Wednesday evening, by the Rev. Dr. Keith, Mr. Robert Maxwell, Factor, to Miss Mary Huxham, both of this city. (Friday, December 7, 1804.)

Married, on Sunday evening last, by the Rev. Mr. Munds, Mr. Elisha Catlett, to Mrs. Margaret Jennings. (Sat., Dec. 15, 1804.)

—, on Thursday evening, by the Rev. Mr. M'Culloch, Mr. William Presly, to Miss Eliza Eleanor Adams, daughter of Mr. David Adams, Factor.
—, same evening, by the Rev. Mr. Munds, Mr. George Jones, to Miss Elizabeth Murdoch, both of this place. (Saturday, December 15, 1804.)

Married, on Wednesday evening last, by the Rev. Mr. Keith, Mr. James Graves, of St. Bartholomew's Parish, to Miss Sarah Minott, of this city. (Saturday, December 22, 1804.)

Married, at Santee, on Thursday the 13th instant, Mr. John C. Schultz, merchant, of Columbia, to Miss Sarah Flud Canty. (Thursday, December 27, 1804.)

Married, in St. Bartholomew's Parish, the 18th inst. by the Rev. Mr. Floyd, Doctor John Oswald, to Miss Keziah Walter, daughter of Jacob Walter, Esq.
Married, on Sunday evening last, by the Rev. Dr. Buist, Mr. Daniel Stewart, to Mrs. Sarah Mallison, both of this city. (Friday, December 28, 1804.)

Married, on the 11th inst. in St. John's Parish, by the Rev. Mr. Pogson, Dr. Philip G. Prioleau, to Miss Catharine Cordes.
Married, on Thursday evening last, by the Rev. Mr. Munds, Mr. Joseph Mulligan, to Miss Jane Simms, both of this city. (Saturday, December 29, 1804.)

Married, by the Rev. Mr. Darley, on Thursday the 27th December last, Benjamin Fisher, Esq. to the amiable Miss Mary Koger, eldest daughter of Captain Joseph Koger, of Saint Bartholomew's.
Married, on New-Year's evening, by the Rev. Dr. Jenkins, Mr. John Dougherty, stucco plaisterer, to Miss Margaret Borrow, both of this city.
Married, on New-Year's evening, by the Rev. Dr. Furman, Mr. David Kettleband, to Miss Margaret Hussey, both of this city.
Married, on Monday evening last, by the Rev. Dr. Keith, Mr. John S. Bennett, to Miss Ann B. Keith.
Married, on Tuesday evening, by the Rev. Dr. Hollingshead, Mr. Josiah Rhodus, of Wadmalaw, to Mrs. Rebecca Humphreys, of John's Island. (Thursday, January 3, 1805.)

Married, on the 25th December last, by the Rev. Dr. O'Farrell, Mr. George Robertson, of this city, to Miss Mary Mis-Campbell, daughter of Mr. James Mis-Campbell, of Santee. (Thursday, January 3, 1805.)

Married, on Thursday evening, by the Rev. Dr. Hollingshead, Mr. Thomas Sheppard, one of the Editors of the *Times*, to Miss Christiana Coates.
Married, on Sunday evening, by the Rev. Mr. Munds, Mr. George Dunscombe, to Miss Sarah Campbell, both of this place.
Married, on Thursday evening, by the Rev. Mr. Munds, Mr. William Linds, to Miss Harriet Fair, both of this place.
Married, on Thursday evening, by the Rev. Mr. Price, Mr. Charles Holmes, to the amiable Miss Eliza Margaret Harvey, daughter of Capt. Benjamin Harvey, of this place. (Saturday, January 5, 1805.)

Married on the 13th of November last, by the Rev. Mr. M'Culler, Mr. George Washington Chinners, of this city, to Miss Sarah Ann Elizabeth Chinners, of St. John's, Berkley county.
Married, on Friday evening last, by the Rev. Dr. Jenkins, Mr. Nathaniel Pike, Stucco Plaisterer, to the amiable Miss Mary Turner, both of this city. (Monday, January 7, 1805.)

Married, on Sunday evening, by the Rev. Dr. Buist, Mr. Archibald Bubner, to Miss Margaret D. Rowland, both of this city. (Tuesday, January 8, 1805.)

Married, on Tuesday evening, by the Rev. Dr. Jenkins, Thomas Hunt, Esq. to Miss Gaillard, daughter of John Gaillard, Esq. deceased.
Married, at Liberty-Hill, Newberry District, on the 28th December last, Mr. John Blair, of this city, merchant, to Miss Sarah C. Ewell, daughter of Mr. James Ewell, late of Lancaster county, Virginia. (Thursday, January 10, 1805.)

Married, at Georgetown, on Tuesday the 1st instant, by the Rev. Mr. Botsford, Mr. George Washington Heriot, to Miss Eliza Fuchey, both of that town. (Saturday, January 12, 1805.)

Married, on Sunday evening, on Edisto Island, by the Rev. Donald M'Leod, Mr. James Mair, of this city, to Miss Martha Graham, youngest daughter of the Rev. Wm. E. Graham, deceased. (Tuesday, January 15, 1805.)

Married on the 22d of October last, at Malton, (Eng.) Mr. R. Wood, of the Blue Ball public House, of that place, to Mrs. Sarah Murrill, late house-keeper to John Webb Weston, esq. Guilford, Surrey. We have a notice, that this marriage took place in consequence of an advertisement for "*A Wife*," which appeared in the York Herald in July last. The advertisement being read by the lady's maid, she immediately shewed it to the house-keeper, telling her it would be a good match for her. After some little correspondence, an interview took place at Grantham, and the lady was brought down to Malton, to see the situation. Everything proving agreeable, the marriage was speedily consummated. Seldom has any circumstance happened at Malton which has excited more curiosity and attention;—there is scarcely a person in the town or neighbourhood but has been at the Blue Ball to pay their respects to the bride, who is a very handsome and most respectable woman. Our correspondent concludes—"This modern way of procuring a wife is much liked here, and I doubt not but you will have many more applications of the kind."—*York Herald.* (Wednesday, January 16, 1805.)

Married, on the first instant, Mr. Peter Gaillard, jun. of St. Stephen's Parish, to Miss Elizabeth Gourdin, eldest daughter of Theodore Gourdin, Esq.
Married, on the first of November last, in the state of New York, Rufus Smith, Esq. to the amiable Miss Sally Wales, of Connecticut. (Saturday, January 19, 1805.)

Married, on Thursday evening last, by the Rev. Dr. Hollingshead, Mr. Robert W. Cleary, to Miss Eliza Bee, both of this place.
Married, on Edisto, the 21st inst. by the Rev. Donald M'Leod, Mr. Hugh Wilson, jun. to Miss Ann Jenkins, daughter of Col. Joseph Jenkins, deceased.
Married, on Thursday the 24th inst. by the Rev. P. Mathews, John Allman, Esq. to the amiable Miss Sarah Heartman, of Christ-Church Parish. (Saturday, January 26, 1805.)

Married, on the 1st inst. Mr. Daniel M'Mahan, of Pinckneyville, merchant, to Miss Margaret Kincaid, of Fairfield district. (Monday, January 28, 1805.)

Married, on Sunday last, by the Rev. Mr. Mathews, Mr. John Johnston, to Mrs. Ann Smith, widow of Archibald Smith, junr. both of this city. (Tuesday, January 29, 1805.)

Married, on Tuesday evening 29th instant, by the Rev. Mr. Bowen, Mr. Charles Kiddell, to Miss Rachel Alexander, both of this city. (Thursday, January 31, 1805.)

Married, on Wednesday the 23d ult. on Edisto Island, by the Rev. Mr. M'Leod, Henry John Jones, Esq. to Miss Mary Ann Miot, both of this city. (Saturday, February 2, 1805.)

Married, on Sunday evening last, by the Rev. Mr. Bowen, Mr. John Nicholas Martin, to Miss Mary Dorothy Kelly, both of this city. (Tuesday, February 5, 1805.)

Married, on Thursday evening last, by the Rev. Dr. Jenkins, the Rev. Nathaniel Bowen, Rector of St. Michael's Church, to Miss Margaret Blake, daughter of John Blake, Esq.

Communication.

Married, on Thursday evening last, by the Rev. Mr. James H. Mellard, Doctor John L. E. W. Shecut, of this city, to the amiable Miss Susanna Ballard, of Georgetown.

Ye sticklers for honors, and hoarders of wealth,
Ye sportive and sprightly, with youth and with wealth,
Pray trip it to Hymen, and no longer tarry;
You'll ne'er get, nor enjoy, any bliss till you marry:
And only reflect, if you do not soon go,
That when you'd say *yes*, you'll find others say No.

(Saturday, February 9, 1805.)

Married, on Saturday evening last, by the Rev. Dr. Buist, Mr. James Carmichael, of this city, to Mrs. Eliza Evans Johnston, of Savannah. (Tuesday, February 12, 1805.)

Married, on Thursday, 7th inst. by the Rev. N. Bowen, the Rev. Milward Pogson, to Miss Henrietta Wragg, eldest daughter of the late William Wragg, Esq. of Ashley Barony. (Friday, February 15, 1805.)

Married, on Tuesday evening, by the Rev. Dr. Bowen, Colonel William Fishburne, to Miss Mary C. Snipes. (Thursday, February 21, 1805.)

Married, on Wednesday evening, by the Rev. Dr. Hollingshead, Mr. James Freeman, of Wadmalaw Island, to Mrs. Rachael Ravell, relict of the late Mr. John Ravell, of this city. (Friday, February 22, 1805.)

Married, on the 7th inst. at Sunbury, (Georgia) by the Rev. William M'Whir, Henry Harford, Esq. merchant, of Darien, to Mrs. Esther Dean Fabian. (Monday, February 25, 1805.)

Married on Sunday evening, by the Rev. Mr. Levrier, Mr. John Schirer, to Miss Eliza Galler. (Tuesday, March 5, 1805.)

Married on Friday evening last, Mr. J. H. Fashender, to Miss Margaret M'La Henderson, both of Delemhorst, Germany.[1] (Tuesday, March 12, 1805.)

Married, at Camden, (S. C.) on Thursday evening, the 7th inst. by the Rev. John M. Roberts, Mr. Jonathan Eccles, Merchant, to the amiable Miss Catharine Thornton, both of that place. (Wednesday, March 13, 1805.)

Married, on Thursday evening last, in Statesburg, by the Rev. Mr. Jones, Mr. James Monk, Silversmith and Watch-maker, of this city, to Miss Jane Campbell, of Statesburg. (Thursday, March 14, 1805.)

Married on Sunday evening last, by the Rev. Dr. Jenkins, Mr. Richard Haged, to Miss Henrietta Donnavan, both of this city. (Tuesday, March 19, 1805.)

[1]A Paragraph relating to a marriage, having been incorrectly stated yesterday, we have been requested to give the following a place.
Married, on Saturday last, by the Rev. Israel Munds, Mr. John H. Fashender, to Miss Marcareta Magdalena Heinrichs, of Delmenhorst, Germany. (Wednesday, March 13, 1805.)

Married on Tuesday last, by the Rev. Israel Munds, Mr. William Lewis, to Mrs. Barbara Amelia Thompson, residing near Jacksonborough, St. Bartholomew's parish. (Saturday, March 23, 1805.)

Married, on Thursday evening last, by the Rev. Dr. Hollingshead, Mr. Mathew Miller, to Miss Rose-Ann May.
Married, on Sunday evening last, by the Rev. Dr. Furman, Dr. S. N. Niderburgh, to Mrs. Mary Reynolds. (Wednesday, March 27, 1805.)

Married, on Sunday evening, by the Rev. Dr. Buist, Mr. James Pennall, merchant, to Miss Catharine Eliza Smith, only daughter of the late Mr. Andrew Smith, both of this city. (Tuesday, April 2, 1805.)

Married, at Georgetown, on Thursday evening, the 28th ult. by the Rev. Mr. Fraser, John B. White, Esq. of this city, to Miss Eliza Allston, of Georgetown. (Wednesday, April 3, 1805.)

Married, on the 28th ult. by the Rev. Dr. Hollingshead, John Geddes, Esqr. Attorney at Law, to Miss Ann Chalmers, both of this city.
—, on Wednesday evening, by Mr. E. D. L. Motta, Mr. Aaron Moise to Miss Philah Cohen, both of this city.
—, on Wednesday evening, by the Rev. Mr. Munds, Captain Joshua Fisher to Miss Rosanna Fairley.
—, on Wednesday evening, by the Rev. Mr. Munds, Mr. James Thompson, to Mrs. Elizabeth Robinson, both of this place. (Friday, April 5, 1805.)

Married on Wednesday evening last, by Mr. Solomon Hyams, Mr. Samuel Jacobs, to Miss Catherine Hyams, both of this city.
Married on Thursday evening, by the Rev. Dr. Hollingshead, Mr. James Hasell, to Miss Margaret Dawes, both of this city. (Saturday, April 6, 1805.)

Married, in St. Bartholomew's Parish, on Sunday evening the 7th inst. by the Rev. T. D. Bladen, Capt. Godfrey Adams, to Mrs. Jane Hoff, the relict of the late Capt. William Hoff, of the round O. (Wednesday, April 10, 1805.)

Married, on Tuesday evening last, by the Rev. Mr. Jenkins, Captain Charles Taylor, of Alexandria, to Miss Sophia George, daughter of Captain James George, of this city. (Saturday, April 13, 1805.)

Married, at Nassau, N. P. on the 2d instant, Robert Anderson, Esq. of this city, to Miss Maria Thomas, daughter of George Thomas, Esq. late Captain in his Majesty's 6th West-India Regiment. (Wednesday, April 17, 1805.)

Married, on Tuesday evening, by the Rev. Dr. Furman, Capt. Clark Tingham, to Miss Susan Foffler, both of this city. (Friday, April 19, 1805.)

Married, on Thursday evening last, by the Rev. Mr. Munds, Mr. Robert Fisher, to Miss Sarah Byers, both of this city.
Married, on Friday evening, by the Rev. Mr. Munds, Capt. David Leslie, to Miss Martha Cunningham, both of this city. (Monday, April 22, 1805.)

Married, on Tuesday evening last, by the Rev. Mr. Munds, Mr. William John Bryer, to Miss Sarah Miller. (Thursday, April 25, 1805.)

Married, on the 10th instant, by the Rev. Mr. Waddell, the Rev. Benjamin R. Montgomery, of Pendleton, to the amiable Miss Eliza Nichols, eldest daughter of Julius Nichols, esq. of Abbeville.
Married, on Thursday the 14th March last, by the Rev. Mr. Kelley, Mr. William H. Day, to the amiable and accomplished Miss Polley Izard, both of Laurens district.
Married, at Portsmouth, (N. C.) the 6th inst. Mr. John Egleston, to Miss Sarah Morton, of that place. (Friday, April 26, 1805.)

Married last evening, by the Rev. Dr. Keith, Mr. Samuel Parks, to Miss Maria Richardson; both of this city. (Tuesday, April 30, 1805.)

Married, on Saturday the 21st ult. by Rev. Joshua Lewis, Mr. Laurence Prince, to Miss Charlotte Benton, daughter of Col. Samuel[1] Benton, Cheraw-hill, Pedee. (Thurs., May 2, 1805.)

[1] Lamuel.

Married, at Wilmington, N. C. the 18th ult. by the Rev. Dr. Halling, Mr. William Scarborough, jun. of Savannah, to Miss Julia Bernard, of that town. (Thursday, May 2, 1805.)

Married, last evening, by the Rev. Mr. Munds, Mr. John Boyd, to Miss Sarah Legare, both of this City. (Friday, May 3, 1805.)

Married, by the Rev. John Atkins, at Batavia, on the Congaree, on the 30th of April last, Dr. Fortunatis Bryan, to Miss Elizabeth Goodbee DuPont, daughter of the late Josiah DuPont, Esq. (Wednesday, May 8, 1805.)

Married at Columbia, S. C. on the 28th ult. by the Rev. Mr. Nixon, Mr. Edward Wingate, to the amiable Miss Sophia Brown, daughter of Capt. Richard Brown, near M'Cord's Ferry. (Tuesday, May 14, 1805.)

Married, on Thursday evening last, by the Rev. Dr. Hollingshead, Mr. Robert Little, to Mrs. Mary Keen, both of this city. (Saturday, May 18, 1805.)

Married, on Saturday evening last, by the Rev. Dr. Buist, Capt. Alexander Campbell, to Mrs. Martha Cameron, both of this city. (Wednesday, May 22, 1805.)

Married, on Saturday last, at Burden's Island, St. Paul's Parish, by the Rev. James M'Ilhenny, Dr. John King to Miss Mary Burden.
Married, on Wednesday evening, by the Rev. Dr. Bowen, Capt. Jacob R. Valk, to Miss Sarah Gyles, both of this city. (Friday, May 24, 1805.)

The paper for Wednesday, May 29, 1805, announced the death of Dr. David Oliphant, and in the sketch of his life the statement is made that he had married Miss Vernon, of Newport, R. I.

Married, on Thursday evening last, by the Rev. Mr. Bowen, Doctor Moses Bradley, to Miss Eliza Tiebout, both of this city.
Married, on Thursday evening, at Hamstead, by the Rev. Dr. Hollingshead, Mr. Isaac Bouchonneau, to Miss Ann. M. Henrichson, both of this city. (Saturday, June 1, 1805.)

Married, on Sunday evening last, by the Rev. Dr. Buist, Mr. Peter Johnston, to Mrs. Sarah Hughes. (Saturday, June 1, 1805.)

Married, on Tuesday evening, by the Rev. Dr. Keith, Mr. Kinsey Burden, to Miss Mary Legare, both of this city.
—, the same evening, by the Rev. Dr. Hollingshead, Mr. Thomas Mills, to Miss Eliza Humphreys, both of this city. (Thursday, June 13, 1805.)

Married, in the Parish of St. Luke's, on Thursday evening the 6th inst. by the Rev. Mr. Hicks, Thomas Deveaux, Esq. Sheriff of Beaufort District, to the amiable Miss Jane Porteous, daughter of Robert Porteous, Esq. deceased. (Saturday, June 15, 1805.)

Married, on Sunday evening, by the Rev. Mr. Thompson, Mr. John Powell, to Miss Clarissa Maccho, both of this city.
Married, on Thursday evening last, by the Rev. Mr. Mathews, Mr. George Smith, to Miss Maria Wilkins, daughter of the late Mr. John Wilkins, both of this city. (Tuesday, June 18, 1805.)

Married at Beaufort, on Thursday last, by the Rev. Mr. Palmer, Mr. Robert Means, of this city, merchant, to Miss Mary Hutson Barnwell, eldest daughter of the late Gen. John Barnwell. (Tuesday, June 25, 1805.)

Married, on Tuesday last, Artemas B. Derby,[1] Esq. to Miss Mary E. Thomson, daughter of Colonel W. R. Thompson. (Wednesday, June 26, 1805.)

Married, on Thursday evening last, by the Rev. Dr. Hollingshead, Mr. Philip Ling, to Miss Charlotte Black, both of this city.
Married, on Saturday evening last, by the Rev. Mr. Munds, Mr. George Beal, to Miss Martha Davis, both of this city.
Married, on Sunday evening last, by the Rev. Mr. Munds, Captain Robert Long, to Miss Mary Blackaller, both of this place. (Tuesday, July 2, 1805.)

---

[1]Darby.

Married, on Monday evening the first instant, John Ball, Esq. of St. John's Parish, to Miss Caroline Swinton, of this city. (Wednesday, July 3, 1805.)

Married at Savannah, on Thursday the 4th instant, Mr. John M'Nish, to Miss Ann Dupont, both of S. Carolina. (Friday, July 12, 1805.)

Married, on Wednesday evening last, by the Rev. Dr. Furman, Capt. Nathaniel Bingley, to Mrs. Mary Lenox, both of this city. (Tuesday, July 10, 1805.)

Married, on Thursday evening last, by the Rev. Dr. Hollingshead, Doctor William S. Stevens, to Mrs. Hannah Ashe, widow of Samuel Ashe, Esq. deceased. (Monday, July 22, 1805.)

Married in this city on the 6th inst. by the Rev. Mr. Munds, Mr. Jeremiah Jackson, merchant, to Mrs. Ellen Fernald, daughter of the late Mr. Charles Crawley. (Saturday, July 27, 1805.)

Married, on Thursday evening, by the Rev. Dr. Buist, Samuel W. Smith, Esq. Attorney at Law, to Miss Mary Crawley, youngest daughter of the late Mr. Charles Crawley, deceased. (Saturday, August 3, 1805.)

Married, on Thursday evening last, by the Rev. Mr. Munds, Mr. David D. Salmon, of this city, to Miss Sarah M'Key, of Fayetteville, North-Carolina. (Tuesday, August 6, 1805.)

Married—on Sunday evening, by the Rev. Mr. Munds, Mr. John Harvey to Mrs. Eleanor Smith, both of this city. (Tuesday, August 13, 1805.)

Married, on Saturday evening last, by the Rev. Mr. Munds, Mr. Thomas Smith, of Philadelphia, to Mlle Clotilde Boudeaud, of St. Domingo.
Married, on the 29th of July last, by the Rev. Mr. Munds, Mr. John Babcock, to Miss Ann Cooper, of St. Bartholomew's Parish.
Married, on the 15th instant, by the Rev. Dr. Hollingshead, Mr. Clarance Morgan, to Miss Ann Wolfe; both of this city. (Tuesday, August 20, 1805.)

Married, on Wednesday evening last, by Mr. E. D. L. Motta, Mr. Solomon Solomon, to Miss Alice Abrahams; both of this city. (Tuesday, August 20, 1805.)

Married, on Tuesday the 30th ult. in Charlotte county, Virginia, Mr. Perrin Aldey, aged 105 years, to Mrs. Ann Tannesley, aged 90—she is his third wife, and he her third husband.—*Richmond Argus.* (Saturday, August 24, 1805.)

Married, in Hertfordshire, (Eng.) Mr. James Young, a strolling player, to Miss Corinda Boger, a mulatto, with a fortune of 9000l. sterl. Some years since, an Attorney woo'd the fair damsel, but, unfortunately for him, she had a great aversion to a limb of the law. She afterwards fell in love with a young Divine, who, in his turn, declared that the accomplishments of Miss B. however transcendant, could never induce him to form a connexion with a black woman. The son of the sock and buskin thought otherwise, and was very happy to obtain possession of her charms. (Thursday, August 29, 1805.)

Married, on Thursday evening last, by the Rev. Mr. Smith, Mr. James Callahan, to Miss Elizabeth Ford, both of this District. (Letter from Kershaw District, dated Sept. 6th in issue for Saturday, September 14, 1805.)

Married, on Saturday evening last, by the Rev. Mr. Munds, Mr. George Carroll, planter, of Virginia, to the amiable and accomplished Miss Charlotte Allen, of New-York.
Married last evening, by the Rev. Mr. Hollingshead, Mr. Thomas Whitesides, to the amiable and accomplished Miss Anne Jefferds, both of Christ Church Parish. (Thursday, September 19, 1805.)

Married, on Thursday evening last, by the Rev. Mr. Floyd, Mr. Henry M. Evans, of St. Paul's Parish, to Miss Martha Rivers, of James Island.
Married on Thursday evening on Sullivan's Island, by the Rev. Mr. Munds, Mr. Bernard Clarke, to Mrs. Gertrude Rockwell.
Married, on Friday evening last, by the Rev. Dr. Buist, Mr. William Scott, to Mrs. Bridget Lopre, both of this city. (Tuesday, September 24, 1805.)

Married, after a *tedious* widowhood of three months, Mrs. Shaw, of the *Recruiting* Serjeant Inn, Halifax, Eng. to Mr. Joseph Thwaite, joiner. It is worthy of notice, that this enterprising and spirited heroine has had three living husbands in the *long* period of three years!
Married at Drax, Eng. Mr. John Harrison, aged 79, to Mrs. Sarah Hembrough, aged 59, his fourth wife—the old man had been a widower *sixteen days!* (Tuesday, September 24, 1805.)

Married last evening, by the Rev. Dr. Jenkins, Mr. Samuel Halman, of St. James, Santee, planter, to the accomplished Miss Agnes Mitchell, of this city. (Friday, September 27, 1805.)

Married, at Petersburgh, Geo. on Thursday evening, the 12th ult. Mr. William M'Dowell, to Miss Sarah Thompson, daughter of Mr. John Thompson, of South Carolina. (Wednesday, October 2, 1805.)

Married, on Wednesday evening last, Thomas H. Deas, Esq, to Miss Caroline Hall, daughter of the late George Abbot Hall, Esq. (Friday, October 25, 1805.)

Married, on Thursday evening, by the Rev. Mr. M'Calla, Mr. N. Hamblin, to Miss Maria Anderson, both of Christ Church Parish. (Monday, November 4, 1805.)

Married, on Sunday evening last, by the Rev. Dr. Hollingshead, Mr. Benjamin Wilkins Ruberry, to Miss Eliza Rhoda Badger, daughter of Mr. James Badger, all of this city.
Married, on Thursday evening, the 24th ult. at Beaufort, by the Rev. Mr. Hicks, D. Archibald Campbell, jun. to Miss Sarah Crawford. (Tuesday, November 5, 1805.)

Married, on Thursday evening last, by the Rev. Mr. Munds, Mr. William Brown, to Mrs. Elizabeth Luscomb—both of this place. (Wednesday, November 6, 1805.)

Married, on Sunday evening last, by the Rev. Mr. Munds, Mr. John Sharp, to Miss Sarah Maria Long; both of this city. (Thursday, November 7, 1805.)

Married, at Orangeburgh,[1] on Tuesday evening the 5th inst. by the Rev. Mr. O'Farrel, George Washington Potter, Esq. Merchant, of this city, to Miss Louisa Ann Lestarjette, daughter of Louis Lestarjette, Esq. of Orangeburgh. (Wednesday, November 13, 1805.)

Married, on the 7th inst. in St. Stephen's, by the Rev. Mr. O'Farrel, Capt. Peter Gaillard, sen. of St. John's, to Mrs. Ann Stevens, daughter of capt. John Palmer, of St. Stephen's. (Friday, November 15, 1805.)

Married, on the 16th instant, by the Rev. Dr. Buist, Mr. Robert Y. Livingston, merchant, to Miss Margaret M'Lean; both of this city. (Wednesday, November 20, 1805.)

Married, on Sunday evening, by the Rev. Mr. Munds, Mr. Charles Corr, to the amiable and accomplished Miss Elizabeth Manson, of this city. (Thursday, November 21, 1805.)

Married, at Savannah, on the 12th inst. by the Rev. Mr. Clarkson, Mr. Thomas Williamson, merchant, to Miss —— Hare of South Carolina. (Saturday, November 23, 1805.)

Married, on Thursday last, Peter Wyatt, Esq. to Mrs. Violetta Peyton, relict of Capt. Peyton. (Tuesday, November 26, 1805.)

Married, on Thursday evening last, by the Rev. Mr. Jenkins, Daniel C. Webb, Esq. to Miss Eliza Ann Ladson, daughter of Thomas Ladson, Esq; deceased.
Married, on Thursday evening last, by the Rev. Dr. Buist, Mr. Josiah Taylor, to Miss Mary Stiles Rivers, both of this city. (Monday, December 2, 1805.)

Married yesterday morning, by the Rev. Dr. Hollingshead, Thomas Mathews, Esq. of White Hall, John's Island, to Miss Harriett Edwards, of this city. (Thursday, December 5, 1805.)

[1]The h to Orangeburgh was officially left off after the Constitution of 1868, the framers of which were but poorly acquainted with South Carolina or the historic names therein.

Married, on Wednesday evening, by the Rev. Mr. Mills, Mr. John Dixon, to Miss Mary Wilkinson, both of this city.
Married, on the 2d inst. by the Rev. Mr. Martin Detargy, Mr. Bernard Litzs, to Mrs. Mary Russell, both of St. James' Parish, Goose Creek. (Friday, December 6, 1805.)

Married, on Wednesday evening last, by the Rev. Mr. N. Bowen, James Brown, Esq. Planter, to Miss Martha Hall Jervey. (Saturday, December 7, 1805.)

Married, on Sunday evening last, by the Rev. Dr. Buist, Mr. John Liddle, deputy inspector of the customs, to Mrs. Roach; both of this city. (Tuesday, December 10, 1805.)

Married, on the 7th instant, by the Rev. Mr. Munds, Mr. George Lusher, to Miss Sarah Mills, both of this city.
Married, at Georgetown on the 5th inst. by the Rev. H. Fraser, Mr. Henry B. Toomer, to Miss Elizabeth C. Shackelford, of that place. (Wednesday, December 11, 1805.)

Married, on Tuesday evening, by the Rev. Dr. Hollingshead, William S. Gibbes, Esq. to Miss Anna Frances Desaussure, daughter of Henry W. Desaussure, esq. (Friday, December 13, 1805.)

Married, on Saturday evening last, by the Rev. Dr. Gallagher, Mr. James Decemp, late inhabitant of St. Domingo, to Miss Laura Prieur, youngest daughter of the late Mr. Prieur, a respectable inhabitant of said Island. (Tuesday, December 17, 1805.)

Married, on Tuesday evening, by the Rev. Dr. Gallagher, Mr. T. Laimable Pezan, to the amiable and accomplished Miss Sophie Hebert; both of Cape Nichola Mole, Island of St. Domingo.
Married, same evening, by the Rev. Dr. Gallagher, Mr. Francois Cormier, to Miss Marie Gospard; both of Cape Nichola Mole, Island of St. Domingo. (Thursday, December 19, 1805.)

Married, on Saturday last, at the Grove, Christ Church Parish, by the Rev. Mr. M'Calla, Mr. Thomas Rodick, to Miss Hamilton; both of the above parish. (Saturday, December 21, 1805.)

Married, on Thursday evening, by the Rev. Mr. Pogson, the Hon. Wm. Loughton Smith, to Miss Charlotte Wragg, daughter of the late Wm. Wragg, Esq. of Ashley Barony.
Married, on Thursday evening, by the Rev. Dr. Jenkins, Percival Edwards Vaux, esq. planter of Waccamaw, to Miss Richards, of this city. (Saturday, December 21, 1805.)

Married, on Wednesday evening last, by the Rev. Doctor Jenkins, Dr. Frederick Dalcho, to Miss Mary Eliza Threadcraft. (Friday, December 27, 1805.)

Married, on Tuesday evening, by the Rev. Mr. Jenkins, John L. North, Esq. to Miss Eliza E. Drayton, eldest daughter of Glen Drayton, Esq. deceased.
Married on James' Island, on Tuesday evening last, by the Rev. Dr. Price, Mr. James Maguier, of this city, to the amiable Miss Emily Barrett, of James' Island. (Friday, January 3, 1806.)

Married, on Thursday last, by the Rev. Dr. Furman, the Rev. Mathew M'Cullers, of St. James' parish, Goose-Creek, to Miss Jane Reddall, of the same place.
Married at Savannah, on the 30th ult. Mr. Joseph Folkey, of this city, to the amiable and accomplished Miss Charlotte Caroline Heinamann, of Savannah. (Monday, January 6, 1806.)

Married, on Tuesday evening, by the Rev. Dr. Furman, Mr. William James Berrie, of Combahee, to Miss Sarah Swindersine, of this city. (Thursday, January 9, 1806.)

Married, on Thursday evening, by the Rev. Dr. Furman, Mr. Nathaniel Cohin to Miss Christianna Brower, both of this city. (Saturday, January 11, 1806.)

Married, on Friday evening last, by the Rev. Mr. Munds, Capt. Robert Fletcher, to Miss Hannah Macleod, both of this city.
Married, on Friday evening last, by the Rev. Mr. Munds, Mr. George Grant, to Miss Elizabeth Sinclair, both of this city. (Monday, January 13, 1806.)

Married, last evening, Doctor Nath. H. Rhodes, to Miss Mary Hamilton, daughter of his Excellency the Governor. (Wednesday, January 15, 1806.)

Married, on Tuesday evening the 7th inst. by the Rev. Dr. Furman, Mr. Wm. Allstine, to Mrs. Rachel Cooper, both of this city. (Thursday, January 16, 1806.)

Married, on the 14th inst. by the Rev. Mr. LeMercier, Rector of the Roman Catholic Church of this city, Mr. Pierre Dile, to Mrs. Eugene Magniant Simonet, widow of the late Stephen Simonet, of this city. (Saturday, January 18, 1806.)

Married, on Thursday evening last, by the Rev. Mr. *Munds*, Capt. Joshua Rogers, to Miss Eliza Maria Ashman.
On Friday evening, Mr. George Darley, to Mrs. Isabella Londay.
On Saturday evening, Mr. Isaac Jones, to Miss Margaret Lowe. (Monday, January 27, 1806.)

Married, on Wednesday 29th ult. by the Rev. Dr. Hollinshead, Mr. Jeremiah Crowell, to Miss Sarah Dewees, both of this city. (Tuesday, February 4, 1806.)

Married, on Saturday evening last by the Rev. Mr. Jenkins, Dr. William Burgoyne, to Miss Eliza Moser.
Married, on Sunday evening last, on James Island, by the Rev. Mr. Price, Mr. Thomas Rivers, to Miss Eliza M'Kinney. (Tuesday, February 11, 1806.)

Married, on Saturday evening last, capt. John Warren, to Mrs. Elizabeth Hearkley, both of this city.
Married, on Sunday evening last, by the Rev. Dr. Hollinshead, capt. William Newton, to Miss Ann Minott. (Wednesday, February 12, 1806.)

Married, on Tuesday evening, by the Rev. Mr. Bowen, Mr. James Fowler, to Miss Mary Eliza Hart, both of this city. (Friday, February 14, 1806.)

Married, on Thursday last, by the Rev. Dr. Hollinshead, Mr. James Washington Brandt, to Miss Mary W. Pepper, of Christ Church Parish.
Married, on Saturday evening, by the Rev. Mr. Munds, Mr. Lewis Harper, to Miss Charlotte Chambers. (Tuesday, February 18, 1806.)

Married, on Sunday evening, by the Rev. Mr. Munds, Mr. Peter Marley, to Miss Laney Thompson.
Married, on Sunday evening, by the Rev. Mr. Munds, Mr. George Scott, to Miss Mary Cook. (Tuesday, February 18, 1806.)

Married last evening, by the Rev. Dr. Furman, Mr. Charles Lawrence, Factor, to Miss Sarah C. Yates, both of this city. (Wednesday, February 19, 1806.)

Married, on Tuesday evening, by the Rev. Dr. Keith, Mr. William S. Bennet, to Miss Ann Theus; both of this city. (Thursday, February 20, 1806.)

Married last evening by the Rev. Dr. Jenkins, Mr. Timothy Sullivan, to Miss Mary Hamilton, both of this city. (Friday, February 21, 1806.)

Married, on Monday evening last, by the Rev. Dr. Jenkins, Mr. Peter Artman, to Miss Margaret C. Hauser, both of this city.
Married, on Thursday evening last, by the Rev. Mr. Johnson, Mr. Nathaniel Slawson, to Mrs. Dorothea M. Luscombe. (Saturday, February 22, 1806.)

Married, on Friday evening last, by the Rev. Mr. Munds, Capt. Joshua Irwin, to Miss Rosanna Mary Bland, both of this city.
Married, on Friday evening last, by the Rev. Mr. Caple, Mr. Daniel Benoist, to Miss Catherine Adams, both of this city. (Monday, February 24, 1806.)

Married in Christ Church Parish on Wednesday last, by the Rev. Daniel M'Calla, Dr. David Jervey, to Miss Sarah Capers, daughter of Gabriel Capers, esq. deceased.
Married, on Sunday evening last, by the Rev. Dr. Hollingshead, Mr. Barnard Farrol, to Miss Elizabeth Phillips. (Saturday, March 1, 1806.)

Married, on Thursday evening, by the Rev. Mr. Bowen, Dr. George Hall, to Miss Ann Dawson, daughter of John Dawson, Esq. (Monday, March 3, 1806.)

Married, at Savannah, on Monday evening last, by the Rev. Mr. Clarkson, Mr. George Haldback, of this city, to Miss Catherine Bass, of the former place. (Monday, March 3, 1806.)

Married, on Sunday evening, by the Rev. Dr. Hollinshead, Mr. Magness Ohring, to Mrs. Catherine Louisa Brown; both of this city. (Tuesday, March 4, 1806.)

Married at Georgetown, on the 27th ult. Mr. Charles Gaillard, jun. of St. James, Santee, to Mrs. Sarah LaBorn, of Georgetown. (Thursday, March 6, 1806.)

Married, on Sunday evening last, by the Rev. Dr. Hollinshead, Mr. Christopher Jordon, to Miss Eleanor Clark, both of this city. Married, on Thursday evening, by the Rev. Mr. Munds, Captain William Miller, to Miss Eleanor Maria Bowen. (Saturday, March 8, 1806.)

Married, on Tuesday evening last, by the Rev. Mr. Furman, Mr. John Porter, of Philadelphia, to Miss Eleanor Gray, daughter of Mr. Caleb Gray, of this city. (Friday, March 14, 1806.)

Married, on Saturday evening, by the Rev. Dr. Buist, Mr. Michael Kelly, to Miss Eliza Kennedy. (Tuesday, March 18, 1806.)

Married, on Sunday evening last, on Edisto Island, Henry Bailey, Esq. to Miss Sarah Baynard. (Friday, March 21, 1806.)

Married at Savannah, on the 12th inst. by the Rev. William Clarkson, Major Abraham Twiggs, to Miss Eliza Mary H. Lewes, only Daughter of the Rev. Stephen C. Lewes of South-Carolina, deceased. (Saturday, March 22, 1806.)

Married, on Tuesday evening last by the Rev. Mr. Pogson, Thomas P. Chiffelle Esq. to Miss Henrietta C. Ladson, daughter of Major James Ladson.
Married, on Thursday evening last, by the Rev. Dr. Buist, Mr. Mathew Mullin to Miss Eleanor Blakely, both of this city. (Monday, March 24, 1806.)

Married, on Saturday, the 22d instant, by the Rev. Dr. Jenkins, Capt. John Nervis, to Mrs. Ann Morriss.
Married, in Georgetown, on Tuesday, the 18th inst. by the Rev. Mr. Hugh Fraser, Mr. Robert S. Hort, to Miss Sarah M. Vaux, daughter of William Vaux, Esq. deceased. (Wednesday, March 26, 1806.)

Married, on Saturday evening last, by the Rev. Dr. Hollinshead, John R. Mathews, Esq. to Mrs. Elizabeth Whaley. (Tuesday, April 1, 1806.)

Married, on Thursday evening, the 6th of March last, in Wilmington, N. C. by Peter Maxwell, Esq. Mr. George Cross, of that place, to Miss Rebecca Brookman, of this city.
Married, on Sunday, the 30th of March, by the Rev. Phillip Matthews, Mr. David Dare, to Miss Ann Brookman, both of this city. (Wednesday, April 2, 1806.)

Married at Wadmalaw, on Thursday evening last, by the Rev Dr. Mills, Mr. Thomas Richardson, merchant, to Miss Sarah Seabrook, daughter of John Seabrook, Esq.
Married, on Sunday evening last, by the Rev. Dr. Furman, Mr. Sam. J. Elliott, printer, to Mrs. Patience Wilcox, of Newport, R. I. (Wednesday, April 9, 1806.)

Married at Cater-Hall, in St. Peter's Parish, on Thursday the 3d of April instant, by the Rev. Mr. Beck, James Jervey, Esq. Attorney at Law, of Charleston, to Miss Mary Postell, youngest daughter of Captain Andrew Postell, of Prince William's Parish, deceased. (Friday, April 11, 1806.)

Married, on Wednesday evening last, by the Rev. Mr. Mills, Major James Miles to Miss Eliza Smith Miles, daughter of Robert Miles, Esq. (Saturday, April 12, 1806.)

Married, on Sunday evening last, by the Rev. Mr. Bowen, Mr. William Milligan, ship carpenter, to Miss Catherine M'Kenzie; both of this city.
Married, at Port Royal, on the 2d of February last, by the Rev. Mr. Hadley, Mr. Felix M'Golrita, to Miss Eve C. Hauser of this city. (Wednesday, April 16, 1806.)

Married on Tuesday evening, by the Rev. Mr. Mills, the Rev. Edmund Matthews, of St. Andrew's Parish, to Miss Mary Ann Teasdale, eldest daughter of Isaac Teasdale, Esq. of this city. (Thursday, April 17, 1806.)

Married, on Sunday evening, by the Rev. Dr. Jenkins, Charles Lesesne, Esq. of Georgetown, to Miss Ann Eliza Sergeant, of this city. (Tuesday, April 22, 1806.)

Married, on Tuesday the 23d inst. by the Rev. Dr. Keith, Doctor Thomas Stock, to Miss Jane Smith. (Friday, April 25, 1806.)

Married, on Sunday evening, by the Rev. Mr. Bowen, Mr. Joseph Simmons, to Miss Elizabeth Morton, both of this city. (Tuesday, April 29, 1806.)

Married, on Tuesday last, by the Rev. Dr. Hollinshead, Mr. William Clarkson, jun. to Miss Esther Susannah Doar, both of this city.
Married, on Monday evening, the 21st inst. by the Rev. Dr. Gallagher, Monsieur Francois Tite Duboc, Merchant, from Havre de Grace, in France, to Miss Sophia Leroy, of St. Domingo. (Thursday, May 1, 1806.)

Married yesterday morning, by the Rev. Dr. Keith, Mr. Sterling Edward Turner, to Miss Susan Ogier, eldest daughter of Lewis Ogier, Esq. (Friday, May 2, 1806.)

Married at London, William Francis, Esq. of Charleston, S. C. to Mrs. Richardson, widow, of Long-acre. (Monday, May 5, 1806.)

Married, on Sunday evening, by the Rev. Mr. Faber, Mr. Christian Koehler, to Miss Margaret Riedfield, both of this city. (Tuesday, May 6, 1806.)

Married, on Sunday evening last, by the Rev. Dr. Buist, Joseph Bellinger, Esq. to Miss Lucia Georgiana Bellinger, daughter of Dr. John Bellinger. (Wednesday, May 7, 1806.)

Married, on Tuesday evening last, by the Rev. Dr. Holingshead, Langdon Cheves, Esq. to Miss Mary Elizabeth Dulles. (Thursday, May 8, 1806.)

Married at Beaufort, on Thursday the first instant, by the Rev. Joseph B. Cook, Samuel Reed, Esq. merchant, formerly of Boston, to Eliza Mary Dopson, of Beaufort.
Married, at Camden, on Sunday evening last, by the Rev. Mr. Flin, Mr. James K. Douglas, merchant, to Miss Mary Martin, daughter of the late Dr. James Martin.
Married, at Camden, on the same evening, by the Rev. Mr. Flin, Abraham Blanding, Esq. attorney at Law, to Miss Elizabeth P. Martin, daughter of the late Dr. James Martin. (Saturday, May 10, 1806.)

Married, at Orangeburgh, on Sunday evening the 4th instant, by the Rev. Mr. O'Farrell, Mr. John Vinyard, to Miss Eliza Elliott Lestarjette, daughter of Lewis Lestarjette, Esq.
Married, on the 4th instant, William Nibbs, Esq. of Cambridge, Attorney at Law, to Miss Mary Mims, of Edgefield district. (Tuesday, May 13, 1806.)

Married, in Newberry district, on Thursday, the 1st of May, Mr. James Fisher, planter, to the amiable and accomplished Miss Cary Glover, both of said district. (Wednesday, May 14, 1806.)

Married, on Saturday evening last, by the Rev. Dr. Jenkins, Mr. John Whiting, to Miss Jane Willis; both of this city. (Thursday, May 15, 1806.)

Married, on Thursday evening last, by the Rev. Dr. Jenkins, William Chaplin Fupp, Esq. to Miss Eliza Hann Edwards, eldest daughter of James Edwards, Esq. both of St. Helena Island.
Married, on Thursday evening last, by the Rev. Dr. Hollinshead, captain Henry Leslie, to Miss Ann P. Bincley. (Saturday, May 17, 1806.)

Married, on Saturday evening last, by the Rev. Dr. Buist, Capt. John Thomas Crout, to Mrs. Susannah Woodell, both of this city.
Married, on Friday evening last, by the Rev. Dr. Jenkins, Richard W. Cogdell, Esq. to Miss Cecile Langlois; both of this city. (Monday, May 19, 1806.)

Married on Thursday evening last, by the Rev. Dr. Jenkins, William Chaplin Fripp, Esq. to Miss Eliza Hann Edwards, eldest daughter of James Edwards, Esq. both of St. Helena Island. (Monday, May 19, 1806.)

Married, on Saturday evening last, by the Rev. Mr. Munds, Capt. Philip Drayton, to Miss Catharine Moss.
Married, on Sunday evening, by the Rev. Mr. Munds, Mr. Alexander Gregory, to Miss Henrietta Moore. (Tuesday, May 20, 1806.)

Married, at St. Andrew's Parish, on the 5th of January last, by the Rev. Thomas Mills, Mr. Joseph Alexander, to Miss Sarah Findley; both of Charleston. (Friday, May 23, 1806.)

Married on Monday the 26th inst. by the Rev. Dr. Jenkins, Mr. Josiah Sturgis Lovell, to Miss Hannah Frances Poinsett, daughter of the late Mr. Joel Poinsett, of this place. (Wednesday, May 28, 1806.)

Married, on Thursday evening last, by the Rev. Mr. Bowen, John Stock, Esq. to Miss Ann Chiffell. (Thursday, May 29, 1806.)

Married last evening, by the Rev. Dr. Hollinshead, Mr. William Austin, jun. to Miss Susannah Ellsworth, both of this city. (Friday, May 30, 1806.)

Married, on Thursday evening, by the Rev. Dr. Hollinshead, Captain John Bonnell, to Miss Mary Ann Yates, both of this city. (Saturday, May 31, 1806.)

Married, on Sunday evening, the 1st inst. by the Rev. Samuel Marsh, Charles Martin, Jun. Esq. Attorney at Law, to Miss Joyse Jane Scott, both of Edgefield district. (Tuesday, June 17, 1806.)

Married on the 15th ult. by the Rev. Philip Mathews, the Rev. Hugh Fraser, to Miss Rebecca Beaufort, of Santee. (Friday, June 20, 1806.)

Married, last evening, at the house of A. Motte, Esq. by the Rev. Mr. Bowen, Abraham Crouch, Esq. of this city, to Miss Sophia Jane Withers, of Wilmington, N. C. (Wed., June 25, 1806.)

Married, on Tuesday evening last, by the Rev. Dr. Gallagher, Mr. Andrew Modeste, to Miss Rosalie Bourg; both of St. Domingo. (Wednesday, June 25, 1806.)

Married, on John's Island, the 25th of June last, by Joseph Rush, Esq. Mr. William Weston, of Wadmalaw, to the amiable Miss Elizabeth Fitz, late of Edisto Island. (Friday, July 4, 1806.)

Married, at Baltimore, on the 24th ult. Mr. Thomas Parker, merchant, of this city, to Miss Rachel Wilkerson, of Baltimore County. (Monday, July 7, 1806.)

Married at Beach Island, S. C. on Tuesday evening, the 1st inst. by Walter Taylor, Esq. Mr. Daniel Neal, Jun. to Miss Mary Nail, daughter of Mr. Casper Nail of that place.
Married at Augusta, on Tuesday evening the 1st inst. by the Rev. Mr. Cloud, Captain John Beale Barnes, of the United States Artillery, to Miss Mary Ann Douglas Hammond, of Augusta. (Wednesday, July 9, 1806.)

Married, last evening, by the Rev. Mr. Bowen, William S. Hasell, Esq. Attorney at law, to Miss Elizabeth G. Tart, both of this city.
Married, same evening, by the Rev. Dr. Jenkins, Lieutenant Robert Roberts, of the U. S. Artillery, to Miss Harriett K. Merger. (Friday, July 11, 1806.)

Married, near Camden, on Sunday evening, the 6th inst. by the Rev. Mr. Roberts, Stark Hunter, Esq. planter, to Miss Elizabeth Boykin, daughter of Burwell Boykin, Esq. planter. (Wednesday, July 16, 1806.)

Married, on Tuesday the 8th inst. on Santee, by the Rev. Mr. Reame, Dr. Philip Carolan, to Mrs. Mary Davis; both of that place. (Friday, July 18, 1806.)

Married on Tuesday evening, by the Rev. Dr. Keith, Mr. Christian Reynolds, to Mrs. Elizabeth Culliatt; both of this city. (Thursday, July 31, 1806.)

Married, in Columbia, on Tuesday evening the 25th inst. by the Rev. Dr. Maxey, Mr. E. Hammond, Professor of the South-Carolina College, to Miss Catharine Fox Spann. (Friday, August 1, 1806.)

Married, at Wilmington, (N. C.) on Sunday, the 27th ult. Mr. Michael Delaney, of this city, to Miss Fanny Williams, of North Carolina. (Tuesday, August 5, 1806.)

Married, on Thursday evening, by the Rev. Dr. Keith, Dr. Daniel Legare, to Miss Elizabeth Martha Jones, both of this city. (Saturday, August 9, 1806.)

Married, in Baltimore, on the 31st ult. Jacob Myers, Esq. of Georgetown, S. C. to Miss Miriam Etting, daughter of Mr. Solomon Etting, merchant. (Thursday, August 14, 1806.)

Married, on Saturday evening last, by the Rev. Dr. Gallagher, Mr. Firmin Follin, to the amiable Miss Victorie Hebert, both of Cape Nicola Mole, Island of St. Domingo. (Saturday, August 16, 1806.)

Married, on Thursday evening, by the Rev. Dr. Gallaghar, Mr. Salem Roe, to Miss Mary Demesey; both of this city. (Monday, August 18, 1806.)

Married, at Columbia, on Thursday evening last, by the Rev. Doctor Maxcy, Mr. John M. Creyon, Merchant, to Miss Kitty M'Call, both of this town.
Married, at Black-Swamp, (S. C.) by the Rev. Mr. Scott, Mr. Nathaniel Polhill, to the amiable Miss Eliza Saint John[1] Singleton, of that place. (Wednesday, August 27, 1806.)

Married at Newport, R. I. on the 8th inst. Mr. William A. Allston, to Miss Mary Young, both of South-Carolina. (Saturday. August 30, 1806.)

Married, by the Rev. Mr. Munds, Mr. Thomas Humon to Miss Catherine Martin, both of this place. (Tuesday, Sept., 2, 1806.)

[1]St. John.

Married, last Saturday, by the Rev. Mr. Munds, Mr. Thomas William Shaw, to Miss Sarah Young, both of this place. (Tuesday, September 2, 1806.)

Married, at Falmouth, (Mass.) on the 21st ult. by the Rev. Mr. Lincoln, Mr. David W. Gillison, of South-Carolina, to the amiable Miss Emmaan Swift, of that place. (Thursday, September 4, 1806.)

Married in this city, by the Rev. Mr. Bowen, Mr. Thomas M'Millan to Miss Elizabeth Godfrey. (Wednesday, September 10, 1806.)

Married at Bombay, D. D. Inglis, Esq. of the Honourable East-India Company's civil establishment, to Miss Money, daughter of the late Wm. Money, Esq. of Walthamshire, Essex. (Wednesday, September 24, 1806.)

Married, on the 30th ult. at Saratoga, state of New-York, by the Rev. J. Van Horn, John F. Burgwin, esq. of the Hermitage, N. Carolina, to Miss Hunt, daughter of Robert Hunt, Esqr. of New-bern, in the same state. (Saturday, September 27, 1806.)

Married last evening, by the Rev. Mr. Furman, Mr. Lewis Groning, merchant, to Miss Hannah Coen, both of this city. (Monday, September 29, 1806.)

Married, on Tuesday evening last, Capt. Edward Walker, to Miss Eliza Teasdale; both of this city. (Thursday, October 2, 1806.)

Married, on Saturday Evening last by the Rev. Dr. Gallagher, Mr. Henry Querard, to Miss Margaretta Sophia Pellesser. (Tuesday, October 7, 1806.)

Married, on the 2d inst. at New-York, Lieut. Ralph Izard, of the United States Navy, to Miss Elizabeth Middleton, both of South-Carolina. (Monday, October 20, 1806.)

Married, on Saturday evening last, by Dr. Hollinshead, John Walton, Esq. to Miss Elizabeth Wily, both of this city. (Wednesday, October 29, 1806.)

Married last Evening by the Rev. Mr. Bowen, John S. Bee Esq. to Miss Charlotte A. Ladson, daughter of Major J. Ladson. (Friday, October 31, 1806.)

Married, on Thursday evening last, by the Rev. Mr. Bowen, William R. Theus, Esq. of Georgetown, S. C. to Miss Eliza Love Lenud, of this city. (Saturday, November 1, 1806.)

Married at Camden, on the 30th ult. by the Rev. Mr. Flinn, Mr. John M'Caa, merchant, to Mrs. Rebecca Brown, daughter of Col. Joseph Kershaw, deceased. (Monday, November 3, 1806.)

Married at Newport (R. I.) on the 15th ult. Mr. Francis Marian, Jun. of South-Carolina, to Miss Maria Peirce, of Newport. (Friday, November 7, 1806.)

Married, on Thursday evening, by the Rev. Mr. Faber, Mr. William G. Faber, to Miss Catharine Clark; both of this city. (Saturday, November 8, 1806.)

Married, on Monday evening last, by the Rev. Dr. Hollinshead, John S. Cogdell, Esq. to Miss Maria Gilchrist, daughter of Adam Gilchrist, Esq. both of this city.
Married, on the 9th inst. by the Rev. Dr. Buist, Mr. Robert Swan, to Mrs. Hannah Johnson; both of this city. (Wednesday, November 12, 1806.)

Married on Saturday the 15th inst. by the Rev. Dr. Buist, Mr. John Fair, to Miss Catharine Miller. (Tuesday, November 18, 1806.)

Married at Augusta, the 9th inst. by Thomas Cobb, Esq. Mr. Joshua Key, Merchant, of Campbellton, South-Carolina, to Miss Eliza Tankersley, daughter of John Tankersley, Esq. of Columbia County, Georgia. (Saturday, November 22, 1806.)

Married, on Thursday evening last, by the Rev. Mr. Munds, Mr. Thomas F. Quinn, to Miss Mary Elizabeth Gready, both of this city. (Monday, November 24, 1806.)

Married, on Saturday evening last, by the Rev. Dr. Buist, Mr. Robert Eason, shipwright, to Miss Isabella Jane Grassel, both of this city. (Monday, November 24, 1806.)

Married, on Saturday evening, by the Rev. Dr. Buist. Mr. I Charles Hentz, a native of Bremen, to Miss Margaretta C. Henry, of this city. (Monday, December 1, 1806.)

Married, on Tuesday last, by the Rev. Mr. Bowen, Mr. Joseph Taylor, to Mrs. Mary Willis; both of this city. (Thursday, December 4, 1806.)

Married, on Thursday evening, by the Rev. Dr. Hollinshead, Mr. James Clark, to Miss Sarah Mikell; both of Edisto Island. (Saturday, December 6, 1806.)

Married, on Saturday evening, by the Rev. Mr. Munds, Capt. Robert Fisher, to Miss Hannah Ingraham, both of Philadelphia. (Monday, December 8, 1806.)

Married, on Sunday evening, by the Rev. Dr. Gallagher, Mr. Benjamin Fordham, to Miss Eleanor F. Vanderherchen; both of this city. (Tuesday, December 9, 1806.)

Married on the 27th ult. at New-River, by the Rev. Mr. Beck, Joseph Adams Scott, Esq. of Savannah, to Miss Mary McNish, of South Carolina.
Married at Savannah, on the 4th inst. Jacob Haristene, Esq. of that city, to Miss — Savage, of South-Carolina. (Wednesday, December 10, 1806.)

Married, on Wednesday evening last, the 10th instant, by the Rev. Mr. Bowen, Captain Charles Muir, to Miss Catherine Davis; both of this place. (Monday, December 15, 1806.)

Married, on Tuesday the 9th inst. in the Fork of the Congaree, by the Rev. Mr. Thigpen, Dr. John Latargue, late of this city, to Miss Ann Wood Hirons.
Married, at Providence, R. I. on the 22d ult. Mr. Sylvanus Keith, merchant, to Miss Margaret Howard; both of Charleston, S. C. (Thursday, December 18, 1806.)

Married on Sunday evening, by the Rev. Dr. Jenkins, Captain William Flagg, to Miss Jane Imer, both of this city. (Tuesday, December 23, 1806.)

Married, on Tuesday evening last, by the Rev. Dr. Hollinshead, Mr. James Davidson, Merchant, to Miss Margaret Eliza Cambridge. (Thursday, December 25, 1806.)

Married, on Tuesday evening last, by the Rev. Dr. Percy, Mr. Samuel Haskett, Sadler, to Miss Frances Moore, both of this city. (Saturday, December 27, 1806.)

Married, at Winnsborough, on Tuesday the 16th inst. by the Rev. Mr. Reid, Mr. Robert Bones, of Newberry district, to Miss Elizabeth P. Yongue, daughter of the Rev. Samuel W. Yongue, of Fairfield district. (Tuesday, December 30, 1806.)

Married, on Sunday evening last, at Saltcatcher, Mr. Henry Fickling, of Wadmalaw Island, to Miss Wilkie Frampton, of Saltcatcher.[1] (Wednesday, December 31, 1806.)

Married on Edisto Island, on the 25th ult. by the Rev. Mr. M'Leod, Mr. Robert Eason, to Miss Martha Miot, both of this city. (Tuesday, January 6, 1807.)

Married on Monday evening, by the Rev. Dr. Hollinshead, Mr. Thomas Cormick, to Mrs. Mary Carew, both of this city. (Thursday, January 8, 1807.)

Married, at Glasgow, on the 17th November, Mr. H. M. Haig, of Charleston, S. C. to Miss Agnes Ritchie, daughter of Mr. Alexander Ritchie, merchant, of Glasgow. (Tuesday, January 20, 1807.)

Married on Thursday last, in St. Philip's Church, by the Rev. Dr. Jenkins, the Rev. James Dewar Simons, to Miss Harleston Corbett, daughter of Thomas Corbett, Esq. all of this city. (Saturday, January 24, 1807.)

---

[1]Salkehatchie, pronounced Saltketcher.

Married, on Thursday evening last, by the Rev. Dr. Gallagher, Mr. Alexander M. Orr, to Miss Alicia Purfield. (Tuesday, January 27, 1807.)

Married, on Friday evening, by the Rev. Mr. Mills, Mr. James H. Cambridge, to Miss Anne Seabrook. (Monday, February 2, 1807.)

Married, on Monday evening, 12th January, by the Rev. Mr. Munds, Mr. William Clark, to Mrs. Mary G. Marshall, both of the Theatre. (Thursday, February 5, 1807.)

Married, on Thursday evening, by the Rev. Dr. Buist, Mr. William Walton, merchant, to Miss Justina Louisa Gennerick; both of this city.
Married, on Sunday, the 18th ult, Mr. Charles Harris, merchant, to Miss Cynthia Beesly; both of Laurens District. (Saturday, February 7, 1807.)

Married, on Wednesday evening last, by the Rev. Mr. Philips, Mr. William Fair to Miss Margaret Gensel. (Friday, February 13, 1807.)

Married, on Thursday evening, by the Rev. Dr. Buist, Mr. William Scott, merchant, to Miss Mary Boyd; both of this city. (Saturday, February 14, 1807.)

Married, the 1st of December last, at Thorpe Place, Middlesex, (Eng.) John J. Pringle, Jun. Esq. to Miss Izard, daughter of Ralph Izard, all of this city. (Tuesday, February 17, 1807.)

Married, by the Rev. Mr. Sweat, on Thursday the 15th ult. John Heard, Esq. to Miss Martha Wood, both of Barnwell District.
Married, on Thursday the 22d ult. by the Rev. Mr. Sweat, Jeremiah S. Fickling, Esq. to Miss Jane M. Leslie, both of Barnwell District.
Married, on Thursday the 5th inst. by the Rev. Mr. Sweat, George R. Dunbar, Esq. to the amiable Miss Mary S. Fickling, daughter of Francis Fickling, Esq. both of Barnwell. (Wednesday, February 18, 1807.)

Married, at Georgetown, on Thursday last, by the Rev. Mr. Lilly, Mr. Elisha Woodward, to the amiable Miss Esther Lepear; both of that place. (Thursday, February 19, 1807.)

Married, on the 2d of September, by the Rev. Mr. Matthews, Mr. Samuel Roberts, of Bordeaux, to Miss Rachel Jamieson, of this city. (Friday, February 20, 1807.)

Married, on Monday evening, by the Rev. Mr. Bowen, Mr. Henry O'Hara, to Miss Martha Woodcraft, both of this city. (Wednesday, February 25, 1807.)

Married, on Thursday evening, by the Rev. Dr. Jenkins, Benjamin D. Roper, Esq. to Miss Barbara C. Jenkins, daughter of Micah Jenkins, Esq. all of this city.
Married, on the 26th inst. by the Rev. Mr. Charles Faber, Mr. Christian Henry Faber, of this city, factor, to Miss Ann Mary Desel, daughter of Mr. Charles Desel.
Married, on Thursday evening, by the Rev. Dr. Hollinshead, Mr. Joseph Parsons, of Abbeville, to Mrs. Hook, of Hampstead.
Married, on Wednesday evening, by the Rev. Mr. Suares, Mr. Phillips, of Georgetown, to the amiable Miss Caroline Lazarus, of this city. (Saturday, February 28, 1807.)

Married at Ashepoo, on the 5th inst. by the Rev. Mr. Floyd, Mr. Thomas Boone of Christ Church Parish, to Miss Mary S. Jones, daughter of William Jones, Esq. (Monday, March 9, 1807.)

Married, on Thursday evening last, by the Rev. Dr. Hollinshead, Mr. John Cromer, to Miss Margaret Buckle; both of this city.
Married, on Sunday evening, by the Rev. Dr. Buist, Mr. John Mushett, to the amiable and accomplished Miss Margaret Flemming; both of this city. (Tuesday, March 17, 1807.)

Married on the 12th inst. in Prince William's Parish, by the Rev. Mr. Benjamin M. Palmer, of Beaufort, Dr. Daniel D'Oyley, to Miss Elizabeth Maine, only daughter of James Maine, Esq. deceased. (Thursday, March 19, 1807.)

Married, last evening, by the Rev. Dr. Jenkins, Mr. Joseph Couterier, to Miss Emily Louisa Kirk; both of St. John's Parish. Married, on Sunday the 22d ult. by the Rev. Thomas H. Price, Mr. Henry Sterling Rivers, to Mrs. Esther Rivers, widow of Mr. William Rivers, all of James Island. (Friday, March 20, 1807.)

Married, on Thursday evening last, by the Rev. Dr. Jenkins, James R. Pringle, Esq. to Miss Elizabeth M. M'Pherson, all of this city.
Married, on Thursday evening, by the Rev. Dr. Keith, Mr. Thomas A. Vardell, to Miss Susan Phillips; both of this city.
Married, on Sunday evening last, by the Rev. Mr. Munds, Mr. Joseph Norris, to Mrs. Mary Hamilton, both of this city. (Saturday, March 21, 1807.)

Married, on Tuesday evening, by the Rev. Mr. Faber, Mr. Stephen Bulkley, to Mrs. Maria M. Fanning. (Tuesday, March 24, 1807.)

Married, last evening, Mr. S. M. Isaacks, of New-York, to Miss Catharine Cohen, daughter of the late Mr. Gershon Cohen, of this city. (Thursday, March 26, 1807.)

Married, on Saturday evening last, by the Rev. Dr. Buist, Mr. Peter Lanneau, to Miss Rebecca Armstrong. (Monday, March 30, 1807.)

Married, on Sunday evening last, by the Rev. Mr. Faber, Mr. John Burn, to Mrs. Christiana Brown; both of this city. (Thursday, April 2, 1807).

Married, on Thursday, the 21st ult. by the Rev. Mr. Clarkson, Charles Gabriel Capers, Esq. of St. Helena, to Mary Y. Reynolds, daughter of Benjamin Reynolds, Esq. of Wadmalaw. (Friday, April 3, 1807.)

Married, on Tuesday evening last, by the Rev. Mr. Bowen, Frederick Kolne, Esq., to Miss Eliza Neufville.
Married, on Thursday evening last, by the Rev. Mr. Simons, Robert Gilmor, jun. Esq. of Baltimore, to Miss Sarah Reeve Ladson, daughter of Major James Ladson, of this city. (Saturday, April 11, 1807.)

Married, same evening, by the Rev. Dr. Buist, Archibald S. Johnston, Esq. to Miss Agnes Bolton Ewing, daughter of the late Adam Ewing, Esq.; all of this city.
Married, same evening, by the Rev. Dr. Hollinshead, Mr. Nathaniel Black, of this city, to Miss Elizabeth Dewa, of Christ Church Parish.
Married, in Beaufort, S. C. on the 25th ult, by the Rev. Joseph B. Cook, Mr. Robert L. Holcombe, of Savannah, to Miss Eliza Witter, of Beaufort. (Saturday, April 11, 1807.)

Married, on the 19th ult. in Laurens District, by Robert Hutchinson, Esq. Mr. Joshua Hitch, to the amiable and accomplished Miss Elizabeth Compton, both of that district.
Married, at the city of Burlington, N. J. on Wednesday the 25th ult. by the Rev. Dr. Charles H. Wharton, Nathan W. Cole, M. D. to Miss Rebecca Peace, formerly of this city, now of that place. (Monday, April 13, 1807.)

Married, in St. Philip's Church, on Wednesday last, by the Rev. Dr. Jenkins, Mr. Samuel Patterson, to Miss Livingston Smith. (Saturday, April 18, 1807.)

Married, on Tuesday evening, by the Rev. Dr. Hollinshead, Mr. John Gilbert, of New-York, to Mrs. Frances Chinners, of this city. (Monday, April 20, 1807.)

Married, on Wednesday evening last, by the Rev. Dr. Hollinshead, Mr. John Allin, to Miss Elizabeth Baker; both of this city. (Friday, April 24, 1807.)

Married, on Friday, the 17th inst. by the Rev. Dr. Gallagher, Mr. Joseph Perhault, to Mrs. Lititia Atkinson.
Married, last evening, by the Rev. Mr. Jackson, Mr. John Lloyd, to Mrs. Mary Pollock; both of this city.
Married, on the 19th instant, by the Rev. Mr. Roberts, Mr. James W. Murrell, to Miss Louisa Sumter; both of Statesburg, S. Carolina. (Tuesday, April 28, 1807.)

Married, on Thursday last, by the Rev. Dr. Gallagher, Mr. John Courty, to Miss Mary Elizabeth Gauins, both of this city. (Wednesday, April 29, 1807.)

Married in Orangeburgh on Thursday the 23d ult. by the Rev. Doctor Eccles, Mr. Donald Rowe to Mrs. Ann Sabb.
Married, on Thursday evening, by the Rev. Mr. Simons, Mr. Elias Couturier, to Miss Henrietta Couturier; both of St. John's Santee.[1] (Saturday, May 2, 1807.)

Married, on Tuesday evening last, by the Rev. Dr. Hollinshead, Capt. James Cooper, to Miss Mary Broeskey, both of this city.
Married, on Tuesday evening, the 17th of February last, by the Rev. Mr. Hand, Aaron Smith, Esq. of Barnwell District, South-Carolina, to Mrs. Elizabeth Rutherford, of Scriven County, Georgia. (Monday, May.4, 1807.)

Married, on Saturday morning last, by the rev. Mr. Simons, Mr. Isaac Couturier, of St. John's, Santee,[1] to Miss Charlotte Hodgson White, of this city.
Married, on Monday evening last, by the rev. Dr. Keith, the Rev. Mr. Benjamin M. Palmer, to Miss Mary Bunce. (Thursday, May 7, 1807.)

Married, on Wednesday evening, by the Rev. Dr. Hollinshead, Dr. E. P. Crocker, of Georgetown, S. C. to Miss Sarah M. Mackay, eldest daughter of Dr. John Mackay, of this city. (Friday, May 8, 1807.)

Married, on Friday evening last, by the rev. Mr. Simons, Mr. John Marshall, to Miss Maria Medcalf; both of this city. (Monday, May 11, 1807.)

Married, on Sunday evening last, by the Rev. Dr. Jenkins, Mr. John Gros, to Miss Elizabeth Catharine Love; both of this city. (Wednesday, May 13, 1807.)

Married, on Wednesday evening last, by the Rev. Mr. Percy, Mr. Charles Newman, to Mrs. M. Moore, both of this city. (Monday, May 18, 1807.)

---

[1]St. John's, Berkeley, is the proper designation, distinguishing that parish from St. John's, Colleton. Berkeley and Colleton counties were established in 1683, but were disestablished by the Church Act of 1706, which created a St. John's Parish within the former bounds of each of them.

Married on Sunday evening last, by the Rev. Dr. Gallagher, Mr. Charles Spann, jun. of Stateburgh, South-Carolina, to Miss Eleanor Crowly, only daughter of the late Mr. Michael Crowly, of this city. (Wednesday, May 20, 1807.)

Married, on Sunday evening last, by the Rev. Mr. Munds, Mr. John Christian Laudershud, to Miss Catharine Mary Shum, both of this city. (Thursday, May 21, 1807.)

Married, in St. Peter's Parish, on the 12th inst. Mr. James Porcher, to Miss Mary J. Boswood. (Monday, May 25, 1807.)

Married on Monday evening, by the Rev. Dr. Jenkins, Mr. Peter Gaillard, to Miss Rebecca Weyman Foster, only daughter of Mr. Thomas Foster. (Wednesday, May 27, 1807.)

Married, at Fuller-Hall, on Monday evening last, by the Rev. James Simons, Mr. William Lee, merchant, to Lady Belhaven. (Thursday, May 28, 1807.)

Married, on Tuesday evening last, by the Rev. Mr. Faber, Mr. John H. Deubell, merchant, to the amiable and well accomplished Miss Nancy Kercher; both of Savannah. (Thursday, May 28, 1807.)

Married, on the 3d inst. in St. Andrew's Parish, by the Rev. Mr. Price, William Rivers, Esq. to Mrs. Elizabeth Mary Ainger. (Thursday, June 11, 1807.)

Married, last Sunday evening, by the Rev. Dr. Furman, Mr. Robert Roulain, to Miss Sarah Gordon; both of city. (Wednesday, June 17, 1807.)

Married, on Sunday evening, by the Rev. Mr. Bowen, Mr. John Zylstra, of this city, to the amiable and accomplished Miss Charlotte Cordell, from England. (Wednesday, June 24, 1807.)

Married last evening, Mr. R. J. Recardo, to the amiable and accomplished Miss Sarah Hyams; both of this city. (Friday, June 26, 1807.)

Married, on Monday evening the 10th inst. by the Rev. Samuel Marsh, Mr. James Scott, Merchant of Campbellton, South-Carolina, to Miss Catharine Tomkins Key, daughter of Capt. Thomas Key. (Tuesday, June 30, 1807.)

Married, on Monday evening, by the Rev. Mr. Charles Faber, Mr. John Frederick Cutler, to Miss Sally Lee, both of this city. (Thursday, July 2, 1807.)

Married, on Saturday evening last, by the Rev. Mr. Simons, Spencer John Man, Esq. to Mrs. Ann Barkesdale; both of this city. (Tuesday, July 14, 1807.)

Married, on Thursday last, by the Rev. Mr. Faber, Mr. John Pickenpack, to Mrs. Dorothy Schriner, both of city. (Wednesday, July 15, 1807.)

Married last evening, by Mr. Abraham Alexander, Sen. Mr. M. L. Henry, to the amiable and accomplished Miss Miriam Solomons, of Georgetown. (Thursday, July 16, 1807.)

Married, on Sunday evening, by the Rev. Dr. Gallagher, Mr. Thomas Duggan, to Miss Jane Cleyton, both of this city. (Tuesday, July 28, 1807.)

Married, on Tuesday evening, by the Rev. Dr. Hollinshead, Mr. George A. Z. Smith, to Miss Ann Eliza Withers, daughter of Captain John Withers.
Married, at Camden, on the 15th instant, by the Rev. Mr. Isaac Smith, Dr. Isaac Alexander, of the above place, to the amiable Miss Sarah Thompson, late of New-York. (Thursday, July 30, 1807.)

Married, on the 3d inst. by the Rev. Mr. C. Faber, Mr. John Philip Happoldt to Mrs. Elizabeth Flagg. (Wednesday, August 5, 1807.)

Married, on the 13th ult. at the seat of Mrs. Izard, near Haerlem, (New-York) by the Rev. Mr. Wilkins, Mr. Lewis Morris, jun. of Charleston, S. C. to Miss Elizabeth Manigault, of the same place. (Thursday, August 6, 1807.)

Married, Friday evening, by the Rev. Dr. Hollinshead, Mr. John Streather Glen, of this city planter, to Miss Sarah Ann Cole, of Christ Church Parish. (Saturday, August 15, 1807.)

Married, on Saturday evening last, by the Rev. Dr. Buist, Captain John Caruth to Miss Ann Louisa Marsh; both of this city. (Monday, August 17, 1807.)

Married, on Sunday evening last, by the Rev. Dr. Hollinshead, Mr. Noah D. Baker to the amiable Miss Martha Christian; both of this city. (Tuesday, August 18, 1807.)

Married, at New-York 17th inst. Mr. Wm. Smith, merchant, of Charleston, S. C. to Miss Mary M'Knight, daughter of the Rev. Dr. John M'Knight, of that city.
Married on the 25th inst. by the Rev. Marin Detarguy, Mr. Joseph Finch, to Miss Catherine Spencer; both of this place. (Thursday, August 27, 1807.)

Married, on Wednesday evening last, Mr. Hyam Abendanone, of the Island of St. Thomas, to Miss Grace Abendanone, of this city.
Married, on the 13th ult. in Laurens district, by John A. Elmore, Esq. Charles Ferguson, Esq. to Miss Elizabeth Baizley. (Friday, September 18, 1807.)

Married, on Thursday evening last, by the Rev. Dr. Hollingshead, Mr. Archibald Whitney, to Miss Mary Drennes, only daughter of Mr. George Drennes, deceased, both of this city. (Saturday, September 26, 1807.)

Married, on Tuesday morning 22d inst. by the Rev. James D. Simons, Charles D. Simons, Esq. to Miss Sarah Barksdale, youngest daughter of Thomas Barksdale, Esq. deceased. (Tuesday, September 29, 1807.)

Married, by James Addison, Esq. Mr. Joshua Ripault, to Miss Martha Bunch, of Broughton-Hall, St. John's Parish. (Monday, October 5, 1807.)

Married at Savannah, on Wednesday evening last, Joshua Aydilott, of this city, to Miss Tabitha Bell Edwards, of that place. (Monday, October 12, 1807.)

Married, at Paris, on the 27th of August last, Mr. Benjamin Strobel, merchant, of this city, to Miss Sarah Russell Church, of Boston. (Wednesday, October 14, 1807.)

Married, on Thursday, by the Rev. Mr. Simons, Mr. John Gabeau, of this city, to Miss Susannah Hartman, of Christ Church Parish. (Saturday, October 17, 1807.)

Married, on Saturday evening last, by the Rev. Mr. Hollinshead, Mr. Peter Guyon, to Ann Paterson; both of this city. (Friday, October 23, 1807.)

Married, on Thursday evening, by the Rev. Dr. Furman, Mr. John T. Lacey, to Miss Mary Hughes; both of this city. (Saturday, October 24, 1807.)

Married on Thursday evening, by the Rev. Mr. Charles Faber, Mr. Frederick Naser, to Miss Ann Custer, daughter of Mr. James Custer, all of this city. (Saturday, October 31, 1807.)

Married, on Thursday evening the 22d ult. by the Rev. Mr. Jones, Mr. Patrick Ardagh, to Miss Charlotte Richardson, daughter of Mr. David Richardson, of Richardsonville, Edgefield district. (Thursday, November 5, 1807.)

Married on Monday evening, by the Revd. Mr. Simons, Mr. Simmson Williams, to Miss Catharine Duvall. (Wednesday, November 11, 1807.)

Married, on Sunday evening last, by the Rev. Dr. Buist, Henry James Chalmers, Esq. to Miss Eliza Geddes; both of this city.
Married on Wednesday evening, Mr. Josiah Moses, to Miss Rebecca Phillips. (Friday, November 13, 1807.)

Married, on Wednesday evening last, by the Rev. Mr. Gadsden, William Washington, Jun. Esq. to Miss Martha Blake, daughter of John Blake, esq. all of this city.
Married, on Thursday evening, by the Rev. Dr. Gallagher, Mr. James Riley, to Miss Caroline Mayberry. (Saturday, November 14, 1807.)

Married, on Thursday evening last, by the Rev. Dr. Hollinshead, Mr. Thomas G. Riggs, to Mrs. Maria Mulin. (Tuesday, November 17, 1807.)

Married, on Saturday evening last, by the Rev. Dr. Hollinshead, Mr. Henry D. Herron, to Miss Maria Buhanan, both of this city. (Tuesday, November 24, 1807.)

Married on Sunday evening, by the Rev. Mr. Simons, Mr. James Welsman, to Miss Amelia Holwell; both of this city. (Saturday, November 28, 1807.)

Married, on Sunday evening last, by the Rev. Mr. Gadsden, George Warren Cross, Esq. to Miss Mary Man Pawley, daughter of the late Anthony Pawley, Esq. of Waccamaw. (Thursday, December 3, 1807.)

Married, last evening, by the Rev. Mr. Gadsden, Mr. Philip P. Broughton, to Miss Mary Broughton, second daughter of Alexander Broughton, Esq. late of this city, deceased. (Friday, December 4, 1807.)

Married, on Wednesday evening last, by the Rev. Thomas Price, Mr. John Rivers, Planter, to the amiable Miss Susannah Love Rivers, youngest daughter of Mollory Rivers, Esq. deceased; all of St. Andrew's Parish.

Married, on Wednesday evening last, by the Rev. Mr. Jacob Suares, Mr. Nathan Hart, merchant, to Miss Rachel Hart, eldest daughter of Daniel Hart, Esq. of this city.

Married, on Wednesday evening last by the Rev. Mr. Jacob Suares, Mr. Aaron Moise, to Miss Sarah Cohen, daughter of the late Mr. Gershon Cohen, of this city.

Married, on Wednesday evening last, by the Rev. Mr. Jacob Suares, Mr. Hyam Moise, to Miss Cecilia Woolf, daughter of the late Mr. Solomon Woolf, of this city.

Married, on Thursday evening last, by the Rev. Dr. Hollinshead, Mr. Robert Stent, to Miss Rebecca Wood; both of this city. (Saturday, December 5, 1807.)

Married, by the Rev. Dr. Gallagher, on Tuesday evening last, Capt. Cornelius O'Driscoll, to Miss Maria R. Talvande, both of this city. (Friday, December 11, 1807.)

Married, on Wednesday evening last, by the Rev. Dr. Hollinshead, Mr. John Johnston, to Mrs. Elizabeth Granville. (Monday, December 14, 1807.)

Married, on Wednesday evening last, by the Rev. Mr. Simons, Doctor James H. Fayssoux, to Miss Elizabeth Cripps, second daughter of John Splatt Cripps, Esq. (Saturday, December 19, 1807.)

Married, on Thursday the 17th inst. by the Rev. Dr. Buist, Mr. William Birnie, merchant, to Miss Mary Rout; both of this city.
Married, on Sunday evening, by Rev. Dr. Buist, Mr. Nichol Bryce to Miss Mary Elizabeth Scot, daughter of Mr. James Scot; all of this city.
Married on sunday evening, by the Rev. Mr. Faber, Mr. John Michael Miller, to Miss Sarah Armstrong; both of this city. (Tuesday, December 22, 1807.)

Married, on Sunday evening last, by the Rev. Dr. Buist, Mr. Samuel Smith, Jun. to Miss Jane M'Cliesh; both of this city.
Married in Philadelphia, on the 10th inst. by the Right Rev. Bishop White, Mr. Condy Raguet, merchant, (of the house of Condy & Raguet, of this city) to Miss Catharine S. Simmons, daughter of Mr. James Simmons, of Philadelphia. (Wednesday, December 23, 1807.)

Married, in St. John's Parish, on Thursday evening last, by the Rev. Mr. Thompson, James Addison, Esq. planter of St. Stephen's, to Miss Amelia L. June, of St. John's. (Wednesday, December 30, 1807.)

Married, on Tuesday evening, 22d inst. by the Rev. Dr. Furman, Capt. John Davis, to the amiable Miss Jane Bruse Richardson, youngest daughter, of Mr. James Richardson, of the Island of Bermuda. (Friday, January 1, 1808.)

Married, on Thursday evening last, by the Rev. Dr. Hollinshead, Captain George Preble, to Mrs. Mary Thomas; both of this city. (Monday, January 4, 1808.)

Married, on Saturday evening last, at Runnimede, on Ashley River, by the Rev. Mr. Mills, Robert Smith, Esq. son of the late Right Rev. Bishop Smith, to Miss Elizabeth Mary Pringle, daughter of John Julius Pringle, Esq.
Married, on Thursday evening last, by the Rev. Mr. Bowen, Edward Barnwell, jun. Esq. of Beaufort, to Miss Elizabeth Osborn, daughter of Thomas Osborn, Esq. of this place. (Tuesday, January 5, 1808.)

Married, on Tuesday evening, by the rev. John Phillips, Mr. Henry Bennett, of this city, to Mrs. Hannah Wells, of Christ Church Parish. (Thursday, January 7, 1808.)

Married, on Sunday evening sen'night, by the Rev. Dr. Buist, Mr. James Barkley, merchant, to Miss Sarah Flemming; both of this city.
Married, on Tuesday evening, by the Rev. Mr. Nankivel, Mr. Thomas Melrose, of Christ Church Parish, to Mrs. Mary Phelps, of St. Thomas's Parish. (Friday, January 8, 1808.)

Married, on Tuesday, the 5th inst. by the Rev. Mr. Simons, Dr. Alexander Baron, jun. to Miss Elizabeth Ferguson Ladson, daughter of Major James Ladson. (Saturday, January 9, 1808.)

Married, on Tuesday evening, by the Rev. Mr. Hollinshead, Mr. John Fraser, to Miss Ann Mathews, daughter of Wm. Mathews, Esq.; all of this city. (Thursday, January 14, 1808.)

Married, last evening, by the Rev. Dr. Buist, the Hon. William Hasell Gibbes, Master in Equity, to Miss Mary Wilson, daughter of Dr. Robert Wilson; all of this city. (Friday, January 22, 1808.)

Married, on Thursday evening, the 29th instant, in St. Bartholomew's parish, by the rev. Mr. Fowler, Mr. Richard Henry Fishburne, to Miss Martha Eliza Postell, daughter of the late Col. Benjamin Postell. (Saturday, January 30, 1808.)

Married last evening, by the Rev. Dr. Buist, Mr. James Mackay, to Miss Margaret Munro; both of this city. (Monday, February 1, 1808.)

Married, on Wednesday evening last, by the Rev. Mr. Simons, Mr. John Macnamara, merchant, to Mrs. Mary Donnill; both of this city. (Saturday, February 13, 1808.)

Married, on the 11th instant, by the Rev. Dr. M. Waddell, the Rev. Benj. R. Montgomery, to Mrs. Ann Dunlap; both of Cambridge, (S. C.)
Married, at Beaufort, on the 28th ult. by the Rev. Joseph B. Cook, Mr. Thomas Gardner, to Miss Rachel Radcliff; both of that place. (Wednesday, February 17, 1808.)

Married, on Thursday evening last, by the Rev. Hugh Frazer, Mr. Henry Vernon, of Charleston, to Miss Florida Guerry, of Sampit, and at the same time, Mr. James Daily to Miss Judith Walker, both of Sampit. (Friday, February 19, 1808.)

Married, on the 14th inst. by the Rev. Mr. Munds, Mr. B. T. Stoops, to Mrs. Jones, both of this city. (Thursday, February 25, 1808.)

Married, on the 18th inst. in St. Bartholomew's Parish, by the Rev. Mr. Johnston, Mr. John Fitts to Miss Margaret Berrie, daughter of Mr. William Berrie, of said parish, deceased. (Friday, February 26, 1808.)

Married, on Thursday evening, by the Rev. Doctor Hollinshead, Henry Tudor Farmer, Esq. to Miss Ann Coates. (Saturday, February 27, 1808.)

Married, on Sunday the 21st inst. by the Rev. Charles Faber, Mr. John C. Martin, to Miss Ann Nauman; all of this city. (Monday, February 29, 1808.)

Married on Monday evening last, by the Rev. Dr. Keith, Capt. John Cooper, to Miss Julia Ann Mumford, both of this city. (Friday, March 4, 1808.)

Married, on Thursday evening, by the Rev. Mr. Bowen, Captain John F. Brooks, to Mrs. Jane Bishop; all of this city.
Married, on Sunday, the 14th February, by the Rev. John Yeomans, Reuben Roberds, Esq. to the amiable Miss Margaret Ball, daughter of Sampson Ball, Esq. both of Beaufort district.
Married, on James Island, on the 3d instant, by the Rev. Mr. Price, David Raburn, to Mrs. Martha Nelson; both of said island. (Saturday, March 5, 1808.)

Married, on Tuesday evening last, in St. Bartholomew's Parish, by the Rev. Mr. Fowler, John Miles, Esq. of this city, to Miss Susan Allison Braly, of said Parish.
Married, on Sunday last, by the Rev. Mr. Simons, Mr. Henry M'Kenzie, of this city, to Miss Ann Maria Smith, of Europe. (Friday, March 11, 1808.)

Married, on the 7th inst. in St. George's Parish, by the Rev. Doctor Gates, Mr. William Winter Simmons, planter, of said Parish, to Miss Sarah Joyce M'Nellage, of Christ Church Parish. (Monday, March 14, 1808.)

Married on Thursday, last by the Rev. Mr. Bowen, Mr. John Jennings, of Maryland, to Mrs. Mary-Ann Burges, of this city. (Tuesday, March 15, 1808.)

Married on the 9th ult. by the Rev. Mr. Palmer, Mr. William Peden, to the amiable and accomplished Miss Sarah Bell, all of Beaufort.
Married on the 12th inst. by the Rev. Mr. Galen Hicks, Mr. Charles Capers, to Mrs. Mary Capers, relict of Mr. William Henry Capers, deceased, all of Beaufort. (Saturday, March 19, 1808.)

Married on the 17 inst. by the Rev. Dr. Hollinshead, Capt. William Brow, to Miss Harriet Murphy; both of this place. (Monday, March 21, 1808.)

Married on Thursday evening last, by the Rev. Dr. Furman Mr. Burges Webb, to Miss Catherine Taylor; both of this city. (Wednesday, March 23, 1808.)

Married in Christ Church Parish, on the 22d inst. by the Rev. Dr. M'Calla, Thomas Hinds, Esq to Miss Sarah Hall.
Married on the 24th inst. by the Rev. Charles Faber, Capt. Lewis Strobell, of this city, to Miss Ann Statia Honeywell, of New-York. (Saturday, March 26, 1808.)

Married, on Thursday evening last, by the Rev. Mr. Fowler, Mr. Samuel Jones, to Mrs. Sarah Byrd; all of St. Bartholomew's parish. (Tuesday, April 5, 1808.)

Married, at Beaufort on the 13th inst. by the Rev. Mr. Hicks, Mr. George Logan, of St. Bartholomews, to the amiable Miss Eliza Verdier, daughter of J. M. Verdier, Esq. (Wednesday, April 27, 1808.)

Married, on Saturday evening last, by the Rev. Dr. Hollinshead, Mr. John McKenzie, to Miss Mary Ann Schooler, both of this city.
Married, last evening, by the Rev. Dr. Buist, Mr. Adam Hutchison, (of the house of Jackson and Hutchison, merchants Augusta, Georgia,) to the amiable Miss Elizabeth, Anderson, of this city. (Tuesday, May 3, 1808.)

Married, in Barnwell District, on Wednesday evening, the 13 ult. by the Rev. Mr. Yeomans, James Owens, Esq. of said district, to the agreeable Mrs. Harriett Steads, late of Wadmelaw island. (Wednesday, May 4, 1808.)

Married, at South-Island, on Thursday, the 5th instant, by the Rev. Mr. Fraser, John C. Walter, Esq of Jamesville, to Miss Magdaline Bonneau Taylor, daughter of Captain Samuel Taylor, of South-Island. (Friday, May 13, 1808.)

Married, on Saturday evening last, by the Rev. Dr. Hollinshead, Cornelius Hamlin, Esq. of St. Thomas's Parish, to Miss Jane Gibson, of this city. (Tuesday, May 17, 1808.)

Married on the 10th inst. at Orangeburgh, by the Rev. Mr. O'Farrell, David Rumph, Esq. to Miss Elizabeth Carmichael, daughter of James Carmichael, Esq. (Wednesday, May 18, 1808.)

Married at Orangeburgh, on the 17th inst. by the Rev. Mr. Porter, Mr. William H. Pooser, to Miss Margaret Stroman, daughter of Mr. Paul Stroman. (Wednesday, May 25, 1808.)

Married, on Thursday evening, by the Rev. Doctor Keith, Mr. John M'Fie, to Mrs. Elizabeth Bruse; both of this city.
Married, on Wednesday, the 18th instant, at Walnut Hill, near Beaufort, by the Rev. Mr. Hicks, Richard W. Habersham, Esq. Attorney at Law, of Savannah, to Miss Sarah H. Elliott, of the former place. (Saturday, May 28, 1808.)

Married, on Monday evening last, by the Rev. Mr. M'Quain, Mr. Samuel Chatburn, to the amiable and accomplished Mrs. Frances Duett, widow of the late Mr. Duett, Merchant, of this city. (Wednesday, June 1, 1808.)

Married, in Orangeburgh, on Sunday evening, the 29th ult. by the Rev. Samuel Eccles, Mr. George E. Salley, to Miss Margaret Lockhart Jones, daughter of Samuel P. Jones, esq. (Friday, June 3, 1808.)

Married, on Monday, the 2d ult. by the Rev. Mr. Phillips, Dr. T. P. Cambridge, to Mrs. Eliza T. Motte; both of this city. (Wednesday, June 8, 1808.)

Married, on Tuesday evening last, by the Rev. Doctor Furman, Mr. Peter Larry, of this city, to the amiable Miss Ann Gibbons Chaplin; of St. Helena.
Married, in Northampton county, North Carolina, on the 26th ult. Hyder Ally Davie, Esq. of South-Carolina, to Miss Eliza Jones. (Thursday, June 9, 1808.)

Married, on Tuesday evening, by the Rev. Mr. Faber, Mr. C. F. Matthisen, a native of Altona, to Mrs. I. F. Sandoz, of Marseilles. (Saturday, June 11, 1808.)

Married on Thursday evening, at Mount Pleasant Farm, Charleston Neck, by the Rev. Mr. Faber, Martin Strobel, Esq. to Miss Eliza Martin; both of this city. (Saturday, June 11, 1808.)

Married, in Barnwell District, on Wednesday, the 8th instant, by the Rev. James Sweat, Dr. John S. Fowke, to Miss Sarah B. Johnson, daughter of Richard Johnson, Esq. all of said District. (Wednesday, June 15, 1808.)

Married, on Thursday evening, the 2d inst. on Black Swamp, by the Rev. Alexander Scott, Mr. Robert G. Norton, to the amiable Miss Sarah Mosse, daughter of the late Dr. George Mosse, of that place. (Thursday, June 16, 1808.)

Married, on Monday the 4th inst. Dr. Preeson Simpson, of Virginia, to the amiable Mrs. Martha Latham, of this city.
Married at St. Mary's, on the 30th ult. Lieut. Samuel Elbert, of gun-boat No. 2, to Miss Harriet A. Jackson, formerly of Savannah. (Saturday, July 9, 1808.)

Married, on the 8th instant, by the Rev. Mr. Philips, Mr. James M'Cliesh, to Mrs. Mary Guy, both of this city. (Thursday, July 14, 1808.)

Married at St. Mary's, on Tuesday the 12th inst. Major William Johnston, to Miss Hannah Starrat, both of that place. (Saturday, July 23, 1808.)

Married on the 14th instant, at Manchester, by the Rev. Mr. Roberts, Thomas Polk, Esq. to Miss Sarah I. Moore; all of Sumter district.
Married on the 17th inst. at Statesburg, by the Rev. Mr. Roberts, John B. Miller, Esq. attorney at law, of Sumterville, to Miss Mary E. Murrell, of Statesburg. (Tuesday, July 26, 1808.)

Married at Columbia, on the 21st inst. by the Rev. Dr. Maxcy, Mr. Nicholas Herbemont, to Mrs. Caroline Smyth. (Wednesday, July 27, 1808.)

Married on Sunday evening, by the Rev. Dr. Furman, Mr. George Kimball, merchant, to Miss Eliza Gordon; both of this city. (Tuesday, August 2, 1808.)

Married, on Tuesday evening last, by the Rev. Dr. Furman, Mr. Robert Arthur Baird, to Mrs. Susanna Bunting; both of this city. (Friday, August 5, 1808.)

Married, on Thursday evening, by the Rev. Dr. Hollinshed, John Hancock Woodward, Esq. to Mrs. Esther S. Gantt; both of this city. (Monday, August 8, 1808.)

Married, on Wednesday evening last, Mr. Mark Marks to Miss Kitty Benzeken; both of this city. (Saturday, August 13, 1808.)

Married, on Sunday Evening last, by the Rev. Doctor Furman, Mr. James Haydon Discombe to Miss Eliza Ann Cleary. (Thursday, August 18, 1808.)

Married, on Wednesday evening last, by the Rev. Dr. Hollinshead, Capt. John S. H. Cocks, to Mrs. Arabella Purcell; both of this city. (Monday, August 29, 1808.)

Married, on Thursday evening, by the Rev. Mr. Gadsden, Mr. John H. Willis, to Miss Mary H. Gabeau, both of this city. (Saturday, September 3, 1808.)

Married, on Saturday last, by the Rev. Mr. Munds, Mr. George Durrett to Miss Margaret Wallis, both of this city. (Monday, September 5, 1808.)

Married on Sunday last, by the Rev. Mr. Simons, Mr. Abraham Shoulters, of this city, to Miss Margaret Baker, of Philadelphia. (Tuesday, September 6, 1808.)

Married, on Thursday, the 8th instant, at Coosawhatchie, by the Rev. William B. Johnson, Mr. Benjamin H. Buckner, merchant, to Miss Susan Riley; both of that place. (Tuesday, September 13, 1808.)

Married at Ashepoo, on Thursday last, by M. B. Pinckney, Esq. justice of the quorum, Mr. Willis Hall, to Miss Mary Channel, both of St. Bartholomew's parish.

Married on Tuesday, the 6th inst. by the Rev. Mr. Fowler, Mr. John Gray Green, of St. Andrew's parish, to Miss Ann Catharine Martin, of St. Paul's parish. (Wednesday, September 14, 1808.)

Married in Barnwell District, S. C. on Wednesday evening the 7th inst. by the Rev. Mr. James Sweat, Lewis Scott Hay, Esq. to Miss Harriet Y. Johnson, daughter of William Johnson, Esq. deceased. (Wednesday, September 21, 1808.)

Married, on Sunday evening last, by the Rev. Mr. Pogson, Henry Ingraham, Esq. to Mis Joanna Postell, only daughter of Capt. William Postell. (Thursday, September 22, 1808.)

Married, on Wednesday the 14th ult. by the Rev. Dr. Hollingshead, Mr. Joseph Siebert to the amiable Mrs. Masey Greiner, both of this city. (Friday, October 7, 1808.)

Married, on Thursday evening last, by the Rev. Dr. Hollinshead, Captain Frederick Elsworth, to Miss Mary Elizabeth Burckmyer; both of this city. (Tuesday, October 11, 1808.)

Married on Wednesday evening last, by the Rev. Jacob Suares, Mr. Israel Solomons, to Miss Esther Ottolengui; both of this city. (Wednesday, October 12, 1808.)

Married at Wrexham, Denbyshire, on the 8th September, Thomas H. Hindley, Esq. to Miss E. Meredith. (Tuesday, October 25, 1808.)

Married on Tuesday evening, by the Rev. Dr. Hollinshead, Mr. John Ker, merchant, to Miss Ann B. Perrie; both of this city. (Thursday, October 27, 1808.)

Married, on Saturday evening, by the Rev. Dr. Gallagher, Mr. Edward Dowling, bricklayer, to Miss Elizabeth Ann Cross; both of this city. (Thursday, November 3, 1808.)

Married, on the evening of Thursday last, by the Rev. Dr. Percy, Cornelius Dupont, M. D. of the parish of St. Lukes, to Miss Maria Hutchinson, daughter of Col. Mathias Hutchinson, of the parish of St. George's, Dorchester. (Saturday, November 5, 1808.)

Married, on Sunday evening, by the Rev. Dr. Hollinshead, Mr. Caleb B. Duhadway, to Miss Catharine Hoburn, both of this city. (Tuesday, November 8, 1808.)

Married, on Monday evening, by the Rev. Mr. Bowen, Mr. William Harth, to Miss Mary I'ans; both of this city. (Wednesday, November 9, 1808.)

Married, on Thursday evening, by the Rev. Dr. Hollinshead, John D. Heath, Esq. Attorney at Law, to Miss Eliza Desel; both of this city (Saturday, November 12, 1808.)

Married, at Orangeburgh, on Tuesday evening last, the 8th instant, by the Rev. Mr. O'Farrel, Sanders Glover, Esq. to Miss Sophia Margaretta Lestarjette, daughter of the late Lewis Lestarjette, Esq. (Tuesday, November 15, 1808.)

Married, at Camden, on Wednesday evening the 9th instant, by the Rev. Mr. Flinn, James S. Deas, Esq. to Miss Margaret E. Chesnut, daughter of Col. John Chesnut, of that place.
Married, on Saturday evening the 12th inst. by the Rev. Mr. Munds, Mr. William R. Payne, to Miss Elizabeth Shanweaver, both of this city. (Wednesday, November 16, 1808.)

Married, on Thursday evening last, by the Rev. Mr. Simons, Doctor Henry E. Gleize, to Miss Susannah Peign'e: both of this city.
Married, at Columbia, on the 17th inst. by the Rev. Mr. Bernhard, Mr. Samuel Herron, merchant of this city, to Miss Harriet Bell, of Granby.
Married, in St. John's parish, on Thursday, the 17th inst. by the Rev. Mr. Gadsden, Dr. William Chisolm, to Miss Marian Porcher, daughter of the late Peter Porcher, esq. of St. Stephen's parish. (Wednesday, November 23, 1808.)

Married, on Tuesday evening, by the Rev. Dr. Hollinshead, Stephen Mazyck, Jun. of St. John's parish, to Miss Susan Waring, eldest daughter of Morton Waring, Esq. (Thursday, November 24, 1808.)

Married, on Wednesday evening last, by the Rev. Mr. Simons, Philip S. Postell, Esq. of St. Bartholomew's Parish, to Miss Sarah Dewees, of this city. (Saturday, November 26, 1808.)

Married, on Thursday evening last, by the Rev. Mr. Gadsden, Mr. George Barksdale, to Miss Rebecca Edwards. (Monday, November 28, 1808.)

Married, on Saturday evening 18th inst. by the Rev. Mr. Bowen, Mr. John Gordon, to Miss Elizabeth Serrett; both of this city. (Monday, November 28, 1808.)

Married, on Sunday evening last, by the Rev. Dr. Gallagher, Dr. James C. Moles, of this city, to Miss Eleanor Jacob, late of New-York. (Thursday, December 8, 1808.)

Married on Saturday evening last, by the Rev. James D. Simons, Mr. Thomas Lamb, to Miss Mary M'Donald, both of this city.
Married at Savannah, on the 29th ult. Mr. Joseph Longworth, merchant of that city to Mrs. Elizabeth Leacraft, of Ewhaw, South-Carolina.
Married at New River South-Carolina, on the 1st inst. Mr. Alexander J. C. Shaw, of Savannah, to Mrs. Margaret Stuart, of the former place. (Tuesday, December 13, 1808.)

Married, on Sunday evening last, by the Rev. James Dewar Simons, Benjamin Allston, sen. Esq. to Miss Mary Coachman, daughter of Benjamin Coachman, Esq. deceased.
Married, on the 17th inst. by the Rev. Mr. Charles Faber, Mr. Christian Henry Faber, to Miss Ann Margaret Weissinger, both of this city. (Tuesday, December 20, 1808.)

Married, on Tuesday evening, by the Rev. James Dewar Simons, Mr. Chester F. C. Snow, to Miss Esther Astuin. (Thursday, December 22, 1808.)

Married, on Thursday, the 22d inst. by the Rev. Dr. Hollinshead, Mr. George E. Hahnbaum, to Mrs. Eliza Rhoda Ruberry; both of this city. (Saturday, December 24, 1808.)

Married, on Sunday morning, 25th inst. at St. Philip's Church, by the Rev. James Dewar Simons, Mr. Jeremiah Murden, merchant, to Miss Eliza Crawley. (Wednesday, Dec. 28, 1808.)

Married, on Saturday, 24th inst. by the Rev. Dr. M'Calla, Dr. L. N. Rees, of this city, to the amiable and accomplished Miss Elizabeth Martha Player Legare, of Christ Church, only daughter of the late Isaac Legare, Esq. (Wednesday, December 28, 1808.)

Married on the 24th inst. by the Rev. Dr. Hollinshead, Mr. Samuel Stine, to Miss Barbara Wilson, daughter of the late John Wilson, cabinet-maker of this city.

Married, at Whin Hall, near Glasgow, on the 20th September last, John Nisbet, Esq. Merchant, of this city, to Miss Mary Anderson. (Friday, December 30, 1808.)

INDEX

Abbeville, 21, 44.
Abendanone, Grace, 50.
Abendanone, Hyam, 50.
Abrahams, Alice, 25.
Acton, Mass., 8.
Adams, Catherine, 31.
Adams, David, 15.
Adams, Eliza Eleanor, 15.
Adams, Godfrey, 20.
Adams, John S., 7.
Adams, Nabby, 8.
Addison, James, 50, 53.
Adger's South Wharf, 3.
Advertisement for a wife, 17.
Ainger, Mrs. Mary Elizabeth, 48.
Aldey, Perrin, 25.
Alexander, Abrahams, Sr., 49.
Alexander, Dr. Isaac, 49.
Alexander, Joseph, 36.
Alexander, Rachel, 18.
Alexandria, 21.
Allen, Charlotte, 25.
Allin, John, 46.
Allman, John, 17.
Allstine, William, 30.
Allston, Benjamin, Sr., 63.
Allston, Eliza, 20.
Allston, William A., 38.
Altona, 58.
Anderson, Elizabeth, 57.
Anderson, Maria, 26.
Anderson, Mary, 64.
Anderson, Robert, 21.
Andrews, Loring, 3 (5), 4 (5), 5 (2).
Annely, Maria, 10.
Ardagh, Patrick, 51.
Armstrong, Rebecca, 45.
Armstrong, Sarah, 53.
Artman, Peter, 31.
Ashe, Mrs. Hannah, 24.
Ashe, Samuel, 24.
Ashepoo, 10, 44, 60.
Ashley Barony, 19, 29.
Ashley River, 54.
Ashman, Eliza Maria, 30.
Assalit, Joseph, 8.
Astuin, Esther, 63.
Athens, Vt., 10.
Atkins, Rev. John, 22.
Atkinson, Mrs. Letitia, 46.
Attiner, Ann Margaret, 7.
Augusta, Ga., 7, 37 (2), 40, 57.
Austin, William, Jr., 36.
Austin, Mary Susannah, 13.
Aydilott, Joshua, 50.
Azuby, Rev. Abraham, 6.
Babcock, John, 24.
Badger, Eliza Rhoda, 26.
Badger, James, 26.
Bailey, Eliza, 14.
Bailey, Henry, 32.
Baird, Robert Arthur, 60.
Baizley, Elizabeth, 50.
Baker, Elizabeth, 46.
Baker, Margaret, 60.
Baker, Noah D., 50.
Ball, John, 24.
Ball, Margaret, 56.
Ball, Sampson, 56.
Ballard, Susannah, 18.
Baltimore, Md., 10 (2), 37, 38, 45.
Baltimore County, Md., 37.
Barkesdale, Mrs. Ann, 49.
Barkley, James, 54.
Barksdale, George, 63.
Barksdale, Sarah, 50.
Barksdale, Thomas, 50.
Barnes, John Beale, 37.
Barnstine, Henry, 13.
Barnwell, Edward, Jr., 54.
Barnwell, Gen. John, 23.
Barnwell, Mary Hutson, 23.
Barnwell, 43.
Barnwell District, 43 (2), 47, 57, 59, 61.
Baron, Alexander, Jr., 54.
Barrett, Emily, 29.
Bass, Catherine, 32.
Batavia (Plantation), 22.
Battle of Eutaw Springs, The, 5.
Baynard, Sarah, 32.
Beach Island, 37.
Beal, George, 23.
Beaufort, Rebecca, 36.
Beaufort, 23, 26, 35 (2), 44, 46 (2), 54, 55, 56 (2) 57, 58.
Beaufort District, 23, 56.
Bechem, George Philippi, 14.

Beck, Rev. Mr., 33, 41.
Bee, John S., 40.
Bee, Eliza, 17.
Beesly, Cynthia, 43.
Bellhaven, Lady, 48.
Bell, Harriet, 62.
Bell, Sarah, 56.
Bellinger, B. B., 9.
Bellinger, Edmund, 10.
Bellinger, Dr. John, 34.
Bellinger, Joseph, 34.
Bellinger, Lucia Georgiana, 34.
Bellinger, Mary C., 10.
Bellinger, Sarah C., 9.
Bennett, Henry 54.
Bennett, John S., 15.
Bennett, William S., 31.
Benoist, Daniel, 31.
Benson, Mrs. Jane, 6.
Benson, Major Joseph, 6.
Benson, Lawrence, 9.
Benton, Charlotte, 21.
Benton, Col. Lamuel, 21.
Benzeken, Kitty, 60.
Bermuda, 53.
Bernhard, Rev. Mr., 62.
Bernard, Julia, 22.
Berrie, Margaret, 55.
Berrie, William, 55.
Berrie, William James, 29.
Bevens, Simeon, 14.
Bincley, Ann P., 35.
Bingley, Nathaniel, 24.
Birnie, William, 53.
Bishop, Mrs. Jane, 56.
Bixby, N., 14.
Bixly, Luke, 8.
Black, Charlotte, 23.
Black, Nathaniel, 46.
Black Mingo (a neighborhood in Williamsburg District), 9, 11 (2).
Black Swamp (a neighborhood in Beaufort District), 38, 59.
Blackaller, Mary, 23.
Bladen, Rev. T. D., 10, 20.
Blair, Mrs., 8.
Blair, John, 16.
Blake, John, 18, 51.
Blake, Margaret, 18.
Blake, Martha, 51
Blakely, Eleanor, 32.
Bland, Rosanna Mary, 31.
Blanding, Abraham, 35.
Blue Ball (Public House), Malton England, 17.
Boger, Corinda, 25.
Bombay, India, 39.
Bonaparte, Jerome, 10.
Bones, Robert, 42.
Bonnell, John, 36.
Boone, Thomas, 44.
Bordeaux, 8, 44.
Borrow, Margaret, 15.
Boston, Mass., 3, 8 (3), 35, 51.
Boswood, Mary J., 48.
Botsford, Rev. Mr., 11, 16.
Bouchonneau, Isaac, 22.
Boudeaud, Clotilde, 24.
Bourg, Rosalie, 37.
Bowen, Eleanor Maria, 32.
Bowen, John, 12, 13.
Bowen, Mary, 12.
Bowen, Rev. Nathaniel, D. D., 7, 10, 14, 18 (3), 19 (2), 22 (2), 28, 30, 31, 33, 34, 36 (2), 37, 39, 40 (2), 41 (2), 44, 45, 48, 54, 56 (2), 62, 63.
Boyd, John, 22.
Boyd, Mary, 43.
Boyden, Daniel, 13.
Boykin, Burwell, 37.
Boykin, Elizabeth, 37.
Bracey, Merry, 10.
Bradford, Sarah, 14.
Bradley, Dr. Moses, 22.
Braly, Susan Allison, 56.
Brandt, James Washington, 30.
Bremen, Germany, 11, 41.
Brazier, Rev. Mr., 8.
Broad Street, 5.
Brockington, John, 11.
Brockington, Mary, 11.
Broeskie, Charlotte Henrietta, 12.
Broeskey, Mary, 47.
Brookman, Ann, 33.
Brookman, Rebecca, 33.
Brooks, John F., 56.
Broughton, Alexander, 52.

Broughton, Mary, 52.
Broughton, Philip P., 52.
Broughton Hall, 50.
Broun, Ann, 13.
Brow, William, 56.
Brower, Christianna, 29.
Brown, Mrs. Catherine Louisa, 32.
Brown, Mrs. Christiana, 45.
Brown, James, 28.
Brown, Mrs. Rebecca, 40.
Brown, Richard, 22.
Brown, Sophia, 22.
Brown, William, 26.
Brune, D. I., 8.
Brune, Mrs. Mary, 8.
Bruse, Mrs. Elizabeth, 58.
Bryan, Dr. Fortunatis, 22.
Bryce, Nichol, 53.
Bryer, William John, 21.
Bubner, Archibald, 16.
Buckle, Margaret, 44.
Buckner, Benjamin H., 60.
Buford, Ann, 10.
Buhanan, Maria, 52.
Buist, Rev. George, D. D., 6 (2), 9, 10, 15, 16, 18, 20, 22, 23, 24, 25, 27 (2), 28, 32 (2), 34, 35, 40 (2), 41 (2), 43 (2), 44, 45, 46, 50, 51, 53 (3), 54(2), 55, 57.
Bulkley, Stephen, 45.
Bunce, Mary, 47.
Bunch, Martha, 50.
Bunting, Mrs. Susannah, 60.
Burckmyer, Mary Elizabeth, 61.
Burden, Kinsey, 23.
Burden, Mary, 22.
Burden's Island, 22.
Burgess, Mrs. Mary Ann, 56.
Burgoyne, Dr. William, 30.
Burgwin, John F., 39.
Burlington, N. J., 46.
Burn, John, 45.
Byers, Sarah, 21.
Byrd, Mrs. Sarah, 57.
Cabinetmaker, 64.
Callahan, James, 25.
Cambridge, James H., 43.
Cambridge, Margaret Eliza, 42.
Cambridge, Dr. T. P., 58.
Cambridge, 35, 55.
Camden, 19, 35 (2), 37, 40, 49, 62.
Cameron, Mrs. Martha, 22.
Campbell, Alexander, 22.
Campbell, D. Archibald, Jr., 26.
"Campbell, Donald", 5.
Campbell, Lady Flora Mure, 13.
Campbell, Jane, 19.
Campbell, Samuel, 10.
Campbell, Sarah, 16.
Cambellton, 40, 49.
Canter, Charlotte, 6.
Cantey, Sarah Flud, 15.
Cape, Letitia, 13.
Cape Nichola Mole, Island of St. Domingo, 28 (2), 38.
Capers, Charles, 56.
Capers, Charles Gabriel, 45.
Capers, Gabriel, 31.
Capers, Mrs. Mary 56.
Capers, Sarah, 31.
Capers, William Henry, 56.
Caple, Rev. Mr., 31.
Carew, Mrs. Mary, 42.
Carmichael, Elizabeth, 58.
Carmichael, James (of Charleston), 18.
Carmichael, James (of Orangeburgh), 58.
Carolan, Philip, 37.
Carpenter, Stephen Cullen, 3, 4 (2), 5.
Carroll, George, 25.
Caruth, John, 50.
Cater Hall, 33.
Catlett, Elisha, 14.
Cattell, William, 9.
Chalmers, Ann, 20.
Chalmers, David, 9.
Chalmers, Henry James, 51.
Chambers, Charlotte, 30.
Chambers, Rebecca, 14.
Chanler, Dr. Isaac, 6.
Chanler, Sarah White, 6.
Channel, Mary, 60.
Chaplin, Ann Gibbons, 58.
Chaplin, Silas, 10.
Charleston, The Newspaper Press of, 5.

Charleston Neck, 59.
Charlotte County, Va., 25.
Chatburn, Samuel, 58.
Cheraw Hill, 21.
Chesnut, John, 62.
Chesnut, Margaret E., 52.
Chevers, Mrs. Ann, 7.
Chevers, Richard Holmes, 7.
Cheves, Langdon, 35.
Chiffelle, Ann, 36.
Chiffelle, Thomas P., 32.
Chinners, Mrs. Frances, 46.
Chinners, George Washington, 16.
Chinners, Sarah Ann Elizabeth, 16.
Chisolm, Dr. William, 62.
Chonler, Dr. Joseph, 8.
Christ Church Parish, 7, 17, 25, 26, 28, 30, 31, 44, 46, 50, 51, 54 (2), 56, 57, 64.
Christian, Martha, 50.
Christian, Lucinda, 11.
Church, Sarah Russell, 51.
Clark, Catharine, 40.
Clark, Eleanor, 32.
Clark, James, 41.
Clark, William, 43.
Clarke, Bernard, 25.
Clarkson, Rev. William, 9, 27, 32 (2), 45.
Clarkson, William, Jr., 34.
Cleary, Eliza Ann, 60.
Cleary, Robert W., 17.
Cleyton, Jane, 49.
Cloud, Rev. Mr., 37.
Coachman, Benjamin, 63.
Coachman, Mary, 63.
Coalfoard, Mary Ann, 11.
Coates, Ann, 55.
Coates, Christiana, 16.
Cobb, Thomas, 40.
Cocks, John S. H., 60.
Coen, Hannah, 39.
Cogdell, John S., 40.
Cogdell, Richard W., 35.
Cohen, Miss, 9.
Cohen, Catherine, 45.
Cohen, Gershon, 45, 52.
Cohen, Nathaniel, 29.
Cohen, Philah, 20.
Cohen, Sarah, 52.
Cohen, Solomon, 9.
Cole, Dr. Nathan W., 46.
Cole, Sarah Ann, 50.
Columbia, 8 (2), 15, 22, 38 (2), 59, 62.
Columbia County, Georgia, 40.
Combahee (describes any place on the Combahee River), 29.
Compton, Elizabeth, 46.
Condy & Raguet, 53.
Congaree River, 22, 41.
Connecticut, 17.
Constitution of 1868, 27.
Cook, Rev. Joseph B., 35, 46, 55.
Cook, Mary, 31.
Cooper, Ann, 24.
Cooper, James, 47.
Cooper, John, 55.
Cooper, Mrs. Rachel, 30.
Coosawhatchie, 60.
Corbett, Harleston, 42.
Corbett, Thomas, 42.
Cordell, Charlotte, 48.
Cordes, Catharine, 15.
Cormick, Thomas, 42.
Cormier, Francois, 28.
Corr, Charles, 27.
Courty, John, 46.
Couturier, Elias, 47.
Couturier, Henrietta, 47.
Couturier, Isaac, 47.
Couturier, Joseph, 45.
Cox, Thomas Campbell, 12.
Craft's South Range, 3.
Crawford, Sarah, 26.
Crawley, Charles, 24 (2).
Crawley, Eliza, 63.
Crawley, Mary, 24.
Chreitzberg, Mrs. Mary, 7.
Creyon, John M., 38.
Cripps, Elizabeth, 53.
Cripps, John Splatt, 53.
Crocker, Dr. E. P., 47.
Cromer, John, 44.
Cross, Elizabeth Ann, 61.
Cross, George, 33.
Cross, George Warren, 52.
Crouch, Abraham, 36.

Crout, John Thomas, 35.
Crowell, Jeremiah, 30.
Crowly, Eleanor, 48.
Crowly, Michael, 48.
Culliatt, Mrs. Elizabeth, 37.
Curious marriages, 10, 17, 25 (2), 26 (2).
Custer, Ann, 51.
Custer, James, 51.
Cutler, John Frederick, 49.
Daily, James, 55.
Dalcho, Dr. Frederick, 4, 29.
Darby, Artemas Burnham, 23.
Dare, David, 33.
Darien, Ga., 19.
Darley, Rev. Mr., 8, 15.
Darley, George, 30.
Darrell, Edward, 7.
Darrell, Martha, 7.
Davidson, George H., 9.
Davidson, James, 42.
Davidson, Jenny, 13.
Davie, Hyder Ali, 58.
Davis, Catherine, 41.
Davis, Elizabeth, 6.
Davis, John, 53.
Davis Martha, 23.
Davis, Mrs. Mary, 37.
Dawes, Margaret, 20.
Dawson, Ann, 31.
Dawson, John, 31.
Day, Wiliam H., 21.
DeLa Motta, E., 20, 25.
DeSaussure, Anna Frances, 28.
DeSaussure, Henry W., 28.
DeVeaux, Thomas, 23.
Deas, James S., 62.
Deas, Thomas H., 26.
Decemp, James, 28.
Delaney, Michael, 38.
Delmenhorst, Germany, 11, 19.
Demesey, Mary, 38.
Denbyshire (Derbyshire?), 61.
Desel, Ann Mary, 44.
Desel, Charles, 44.
Desel, Eliza, 62.
Detarguy, Rev. Martin, 28, 50.
Deubell, John H., 48.
Dewa, Elizabeth, 46.
Dewees, Sarah (marries Jeremiah Crowell), 30.
Dewees, Sarah (marries Philip S. Postell), 62.
Dile, Pierre, 30.
Discombe, James Haydon, 60.
Dixon, John, 28.
D'Oyley, Dr. Daniel, 44.
Doar, Esther Susannah, 34.
Doke, Alexander, 9.
Donnavan, Henrietta, 19.
Donnill, Mrs. Mary, 55.
Dopson, Eliza Mary, 35.
Dorrill, Ann, 7.
Dorrill, James, 7.
Dougherty, John, 15.
Douglas, James K., 35.
Dowling, Edward, 61.
Drax, England, 26.
Drayton, Eliza E., 29.
Drayton, Glen, 29.
Drayton, Philip, 36.
Drennes, George, 50.
Drennes, Mary, 50.
DuPont, Ann, 24.
DuPont, Cornelius, 61.
DuPont, Elizabeth Goodbee, 22.
DuPont, Josiah, 22.
Duboc, Francois Tite, 34.
Duett, Mr., 58.
Duett, Mrs. Frances, 58.
Duggan, Thomas, 49.
Duhadway, Caleb B., 61.
Dulles, Mary Elizabeth, 35.
Dunbar, George R., 43.
Dunlap, Mrs. Ann, 55.
Dunscombe, George, 16.
Durrett, George, 60.
Duvall, Catherine, 51.
Eason, Robert (shipwright), 41.
Eason, Robert, 42.
East India Company, 39.
Eccles, Jonathan, 19.
Eccles, Rev. Samuel, D. D., 47.
Edgefield District, 35, 36, 51.
Edings, Mrs. Eliza B., 6.
Edisto Island, 14, 17 (2), 18, 32, 37, 41, 42.
Edwards, Eliza Hann, 35, 36.

Edwards, Harriet, 27.
Edwards, James, 35, 36.
Edwards, Rebecca, 63.
Edwards, Tabitha Bell, 50.
Egleston, John, 21.
Elbert, Samuel, 59.
Elliott, Sam. J., 33.
Elliott, Sarah Hazzard, 58.
Ellsworth, Frederick, 61.
Ellsworth, Susannah, 36.
Elmore, John A., 50.
England, 13, 17, 25, 26 (2), 43, 48, 61.
Essex, England, 39.
Etting, Miriam, 38.
Etting, Solomon, 38.
Euhaw (a neighborhood), 63.
Europe, 56.
Evans, Henry M., 25.
Eve, Oswald, 7.
Eve, Sarah, 7.
Ewell, James, 16.
Ewell, Sarah C., 16.
Ewing, Adam, 46.
Ewing, Agnes Bolton, 46.
Faber, Christian Henry, 9, 44, 63.
Faber, Rev. Matthew Frederick Charles, 9, 34, 40, 44, 45 (2), 48, 49 (3), 51, 53, 55, 57, 58, 59, 63.
Faber, William G., 40.
Fabian, Mrs. Esther Dean, 19.
Fair, Harriet, 16.
Fair, John, 40.
Fair, William, 43.
Fairfield District, 18, 42.
Fairley, Rosanna, 20.
Falmouth, Mass., 39.
Fanning, Mrs. Maria M., 45.
Farmer, Henry Tudor, 55.
Farrol, Barnard, 31.
Fashender, John H., 19.
Fayetteville, N. C., 24.
Fayssoux, Miss., 7.
Fayssoux, Dr. James H., 53.
Fayssoux, Dr. Peter, 7.
Ferguson, Charles, 50.
Fernald, Mrs. Ellen (Crawley), 24.
Fickling, Francis, 43.
Fickling, Henry, 42.
Fickling, Jeremiah S., 43.
Fickling, Mary S., 43.
Finch, Joseph, 50.
Findley, Sarah, 36.
Fishburne, Francis, 10.
Fishburne, Richard Henry, 54.
Fishburne, William, 19.
Fisher, Benjamin, 15.
Fisher, James, 35.
Fisher, Joshua, 20.
Fisher, Robert, 21.
Fisher, Capt. Robert, 41.
Fitts, John, 55.
Fitz, Elizabeth, 37.
Flagg, Mrs. Elizabeth, 49.
Flagg, William, 42.
Fleming, Nancy, 11.
Flemming, Margaret, 44.
Flemming, Sarah, 54.
Fletcher, Robert, 29.
Flinn, Rev. Mr., 35 (2), 40, 62.
Floyd, Rev. Mr., 15, 25, 44.
Foffler, Susan, 21.
Foissin, Dr., 7.
Foissin, Miss, 14.
Folker, Elizabeth, 14.
Folkey, Joseph, 29.
Follin, Fermin, 38.
Ford, Elizabeth, 25.
Fordham, Benjamin, 41.
Foster, Rebecca Weyman, 48.
Foster, Thomas, 48.
Fowke, Dr. John S., 59.
Fowler, Rev. Andrew, 54, 56, 57, 60.
Fowler, Ann, 12.
Fowler, James, 30.
Frampton, Wilkie, 42.
France, 3 (2), 34.
Francis, William, 34.
Fraser, Rev. Hugh, 10, 20, 33, 36, 55, 57.
Fraser, John, 54.
Freeman, James, 19.
Fripp, William Chaplin, 35 (Fupp), 36.
Frost, Rev. Thomas, D. D., 6 (2), 7, 8, 9, 10, 11.
Fuchey, Eliza, 16.
Fuller Hall, 48.

Furchase, John, 8.
Furman, Rev. Richard, D. D., 11, 13, 15, 20, 21, 24, 29 (3), 30, 31, 32, 33, 39, 48, 51, 53, 57, 58, 59, 60 (2).
Gabeau, John, 51.
Gabeau, Mary H., 60.
Gadsden, Rev. Christopher E., 51, 52 (2), 60, 62, 63.
Gaillard, Miss, 16.
Gaillard, Charles, Jr., 32.
Gaillard, John, 7, 16.
Gaillard, Mary, 7.
Gaillard, Capt. Peter, 27.
Gaillard, Peter, 48.
Gaillard, Peter, Jr., 17.
Gallagher, Rev. S. Felix, D. D., 6, 28 (3), 34, 37, 38 (2), 39, 41, 43, 46 (2), 48, 49, 51, 53, 61, 62.
Galler, Eliza, 19.
Gantt, Mrs. Esther S., 60.
Gardner, Thomas, 55.
Gates, Rev. Dr., 56.
Gauins, Mary Elizabeth, 46.
Geddes, Eliza, 51.
Geddes, John, 20.
Gennerick, Justina Louisa, 43.
Gensel, Margaret, 43.
George, James, 21.
George, Sophia, 21.
Georgetown, 9, 11, 12, 16, 18, 20 (2), 28, 32 (2), 33, 34, 38, 40, 44 (2), 47, 49.
Georgia, 14, 19, 26, 40, 47.
Germany, 11, 19.
Gibbes, William Hasell, 54.
Gibbes, William S., 28.
Gibson, Jane, 57.
Gilbert, John, 46.
Gilchrist, Adam, 40.
Gilchrist, Maria, 40.
Gillison, David W., 39.
Gilmor, Robert, Jr., 45.
Givhan, Mary, 12.
Givhan, Philip, 12.
Givhan's Ferry, 12.
Glasgow, Scotland, 42 (2), 64.
Gleize, Dr. Henry E., 62.
Glen, John Streather, 50.
Glover, Cary, 35.
Glover, Joseph, 13.
Glover, Sanders, 62.
Godfrey, Elizabeth, 39.
Godfrey, Mary, 10.
Godfrey, Thomas, 10.
Goose Creek (St. James's Parish), 12, 13, 28, 29.
Gordon, Eliza, 59.
Gordon, John, 63.
Gordon, Robert, 11.
Gordon, Sarah, 48.
Gospard, Marie, 28.
Gosselin, Magdalen, 8.
Gourdin, Elizabeth, 17.
Gourdin, Theodore, 17.
Graham, Martha, 17.
Graham, Rev. William E., 17.
Granby, 62.
Grant, George, 29.
Grantham, England, 17.
Granville, Mrs, Elizabeth, 53.
Grassel, Isabella Jane, 41.
Graves, James, 15.
Gray, Caleb, 32.
Gray, Eleanor, 32.
Gready, Mary Elizabeth, 40.
Green, John Gray, 13, 60.
Greenville District, 6.
Gregory, Alexander, 36.
Greiner, Mrs. Masey, 61.
Griffin, Charles, 13.
Groning, Lewis, 39.
Gros, John, 47.
Grove, The (plantation), 28.
Guerry, Florida, 55.
Guilford, Surrey, England, 17
Guy, James, 6.
Guy, Mrs. Mary, 59.
Guyon, Peter, 51.
Gyles, Sarah, 22.
Habersham, Richard Wylly, 58.
Hadley, Rev. Mr., 33.
Haged, Richard, 19.
Hahnbaum, George E., 63.
Haig, David, 10.
Haig, H. M., 42.
Halifax, England, 26.
Hall, Caroline, 26.
Hall, Dr. George, 31.

Hall, George Abbott, 26.
Hall, Sarah, 57.
Hall, Willis, 60.
Halling, Rev. Dr., 22.
Halman, Samuel, 26.
Hamblin, N., 26.
Hamilton, Miss, 28.
Hamilton, Catharine, 6.
Hamilton, Mary, marries Dr. Rhodes, 29.
Hamilton, Mary, marries Timothy Sullivan, 31.
Hamilton, Mrs. Mary, 45.
Hamlin, Cornelius, 57.
Hammond, Elisha, 38.
Hammond, Mary Ann Douglas, 37.
Hampstead (suburb of Charleston), 22, 44.
Hampton, Ann, 7.
Hand, Rev. Mr., 47.
Happoldt, John Philip, 49.
Hare, Miss, 27.
Harford, Henry, 19.
Harlem, N. Y., 49.
Harper, Lewis, 30.
Harris, Charles, 43.
Harris, Christiana Boston, 6.
Harris, Dr. Tucker, 6.
Harrison, John, 26.
Hart, Mary Eliza, 30.
Hart, Daniel, 52.
Hart, Nathan, 52.
Hart, Rachel, 52.
Hart, Rev. Solomon, 11.
Harth, William, 62.
Hartman, Susannah, 51.
Hartstene, Jacob, 41 (Haristene).
Harvey, Benjamin, 16.
Harvey, Eliza Margaret, 16.
Harvey, John, 24.
Hasell, James, 20.
Hasell, William S., 37.
Haskett, Samuel, 42.
Hastings, Warren, 5.
Hauser, Eve C., 33.
Hauser, Margaret C., 31.
Harve de Grace, France, 34.
Hay, Lewis Scott, 61.
Heard, John, 43.
Hearkley, Mrs. Elizabeth, 30.
Heartman, Sarah, 17.
Heath, John D., 62.
Hebert, Sophie, 28.
Hebert, Victorie, 38.
Heinamann, Charlotte Caroline, 29.
Heinrichs, Marcareta Magdalena, 19.
Heinrichs, Wilhelmina Christiana, 11.
Hembrough, Sarah, 26.
Henley, Sarah, 13.
Henrichson, Ann M., 22.
Henry, M. L., 49.
Henry, Margaretta C., 41.
Henry, Mary, 13.
Hentz, I. Charles, 41.
Herbemont, Nicholas, 59.
Heriot, George Washington, 16.
Hermitage, The, N. C., 39.
Herron, Henry D., 52.
Herron, Samuel, 62.
Hertfordshire, England, 25.
Hicks, Rev. Galen, 23, 26, 56, 57, 58.
High Hills of Santee, 10.
Hindley, Thomas H., 61.
Hinds, Thomas, 57.
Hingham, Massachusetts, 3.
Hirons, Ann Wood, 41.
Hitch, Joshua, 46.
Hoburn, Catherine, 61.
Hoff, Mrs. Jane, 20.
Hoff, William, 20.
Holcombe, Robert L., 46.
Hollingshead, Rev. William, D. D., 7, 9 (2), 12 (3), 14 (3), 16, 17, 19, 20 (3), 22 (2), 23(2), 24 (2), 25, 26, 27, 28, 30 (3), 31, 32 (2), 33, 34, 35 (2), 36 (2), 39, 40, 41, 42 (2), 44 (2), 46 (3), 47 (2), 49, 50 (3), 51, 52 (3), 53, 54 (2), 55, 56, 57 (2), 60 (2), 61 (4), 62 (2), 63, 64.
Holmes, Charles, 6.
Holwell, Amelia, 52.
Honeywell, Ann Statia, 57.
Hook, Mrs., 44.
Horlbeck (misspelled Haldback), George, 32.
Hort, Robert, S., 33.

Howard, Margaret, 41.
Hubble, Sears, 12.
Huger, Ann, 8.
Huger, Daniel, 10.
Huger, Gen. Isaac, 8.
Hughes, Mary, 51.
Hughes, Mrs. Sarah, 23.
Hugoins, Joseph, 8.
Humon, Thomas, 38.
Humphreys, Eliza, 23.
Humphreys, Mrs. Rebecca, 15.
Hunt, Miss, 39.
Hunt, Robert, 39.
Hunt, Thomas, 16.
Hunter, Stark, 37.
Hussey, Margaret, 15.
Hutchison, Adam, 57.
Hutchison, Jackson &, 57.
Hutchinson, Maria, 61.
Hutchinson, Mathias, 61.
Hutchinson, Robert, 46.
Huxham, Jane, 12.
Huxham, Mary, 14.
Hyams, Catherine, 20.
Hyams, Sarah, 48.
Hyams, Solomon, 20.
I'ans, Mary, 62.
Imer, Jane, 42.
Inglis, D. D., 39.
Ingraham, Hannah, 41.
Ingraham, Henry, 61.
Ingraham, Mrs. Mary, 9.
Ingram, Mrs. Grace, 6.
Ioor, Dr. William, 5.
Irwin, Capt. Joshua, 31.
Isaacks, S. M., 45.
Izard, Mrs. Alice (DeLancey), 49.
Izard, Mary, 43.
Izard, Polly, 21.
Izard, Ralph (175.-180.), 43.
Izard, Ralph (1785-1824), 39.
Jackson, Rev. Mr., 46.
Jackson, Harriet A., 59.
Jackson, Jeremiah, 24.
Jackson & Hutchinson, 57.
Jacksonborough, 12, 20.
Jacob, Eleanor, 63.
Jacobs, Samuel, 20.
James' Island, 25, 29 (2), 30, 45, 56.
Jamesville, 57.
Jamieson, Rachel, 44.
Jarman, Harriet, 6.
Jeffords, Anne, 25.
Jenkins, Ann, 17.
Jenkins, Rebecca C., 44.
Jenkins, Rev. Edward, D. D., 7 (2), 8, 14 (2), 15, 16 (2), 18, 19, 21, 26, 27, 29 (3), 30, 31 (2), 33, 34, 35 (3), 36 (2), 37, 42 (2), 44, 45 (2), 46, 47, 48.
Jenkins, Col. Joseph, 17.
Jenkins, Micah, 44.
Jennings, John, 56.
Jennings, Mrs. Margaret, 14.
Jervey, David, 31.
Jervey, James, 33.
Jervey, Martha Hall, 28.
John's Island, 15, 27, 37.
Johnson, Rev. Mr. (Charleston), 31.
Johnson, Mrs. Hannah, 40.
Johnson, Harriet Y., 61.
Johnson, Richard, 59.
Johnson, Sarah B., 59.
Johnson, William, 61.
Johnson, Rev. William B., 55.
Johnston, Archibald S., 46.
Johnston, Mrs. Eliza Evans, 18.
Johnston, John, 18, 53.
Johnston, Peter, 23.
Johnston, Major William, 59.
Jones, Mrs. 55.
Jones, Rev. Mr., 19, 51.
Jones, Eliza, 58.
Jones, Elizabeth Martha, 38.
Jones, George, 15.
Jones, Henry John, 18.
Jones, Isaac, 30.
Jones, Margaret Lockhart, 58.
Jones, Mary S., 44.
Jones, Samuel, 57.
Jones, Samuel Phillips, 58.
Jones, William, 44.
Jordon, Christopher, 32.
Jouve, George, 14.
June, Amelia L., 53.
Keen, Mrs. Mary, 22.
Keith, Ann B., 15.
Keith, Rev. Isaac Stockton, D. D., 6,

10, 11, 12 (2), 13 (2), 14, 15 (2), 21, 23, 31, 34 (2), 37, 38, 45, 47, 55, 58.
Keith, Sylvanus, 41.
Kelley, Rev. Mr., 21.
Kelly, Mary Dorothy, 18.
Kelly, Michael, 32.
Kendrick, Rev. Mr., 12.
Kennedy, Rev. Dr., 13.
Kennedy, Eliza, 32.
Kennon, Henry, 12.
Ker, John, 61.
Kercher, Nancy, 48.
Kershaw, Joseph, 40.
Kershaw District, 25.
Kettleband, David, 15.
Key, Catherine Tomkins, 49.
Key, Joshua, 40.
Key, Thomas, 49.
Keddell, Charles, 18.
Kimball, George, 59.
Kincaid, Margaret, 18.
King, Dr. John, 22.
King, William L., 5 (2).
Kirk, Emily Louisa, 45.
Kirk, Rupert, 9.
Knox, Rev. Mr., 11.
Koehler, Christian, 34.
Koger, Joseph, 15.
Koger, Mary, 15.
Kolne, Frederick, 45.
LaBorn, Mrs. Sarah, 32.
Lacey, John T., 51.
Ladson, Charlotte A., 40.
Ladson, Eliza Ann, 27.
Ladson, Elizabeth Ferguson, 54.
Ladson, Henrietta C., 32.
Ladson, Major James, 9, 32, 40, 45. 54.
Ladson, Mary, 9.
Ladson, Sarah Reeve, 45.
Ladson, Thomas, 27.
Lamb, Thomas, 63.
Lancaster County, Va., 16.
Lance, Lambert, 10.
Lance, Sarah L., 10.
Langlois, Cecile, 35.
Lanneau, Peter, 45.
Larry, Peter, 58.
Latargue, Dr. John, 41.
Latham, Mrs. Martha, 59.
Laudershud, John Christian, 48.
Laurens District, 13 (2), 21, 43, 46, 50.
Laval, Jacint, 14.
Laval, Jacint, Jr., 14.
Lawrence, Charles, 31.
Lazarus, Caroline, 44.
LeMercier, Rev. Mr., 30.
Leacraft, Mrs. Elizabeth, 63.
Lee, Sally, 49.
Lee, William, 48.
Lee, William, Jr., 7.
Legaré, Daniel, 38.
Legaré, Elizabeth Martha Player, 64.
Legaré, Isaac, 64.
Legaré, Mary, 23.
Legaré, Sarah, 22.
Leghorn, 14.
Lenox, Mrs. Mary, 24.
Lenud, Eliza Love, 40.
Lepear, Esther, 44.
Lequeux, John, 7.
Leroy, Sophia, 34.
Leslie, Henry, 35.
Lesesne, Charles, 34.
Lesesne, Mrs. Eliza, 11.
Lesesne, Joseph, 12.
Lesesne, Thomas, 13.
Leslie, Jane M., 43.
Lestarjette, Eliza Elliott, 35.
Lestarjette, Lewis, 27, 35, 62.
Lestarjette, Louisa Ann, 27.
Lestarjette, Sophia Margaretta, 62.
Levrier, Rev. Mr., 19.
Levy, Mrs. Hannah, 11.
Levy, Samuel, 11.
Levy, Solomon, 11.
Lewes, Eliza Mary H., 32.
Lewes, Rev. Sephen C., 32.
Lewis, Rev. Joshua, 21.
Lewis, William, 20.
Liberty Hill, Newberry District, 16.
Liddle, John, 28.
Lightbourn, Francis Stiles, 6.
Lilly, Rev. Mr., 44.
Lincoln, Rev. Mr., 39.

Lindauer, Catharine, 9.
Linds, William, 16.
Ling, Philip, 23.
Little, Robert, 22.
Litzs, Bernard, 28.
Livingston, Robert Y., 27.
Lloyd, John, 46.
Logan, Christian, 6.
Logan, George, 57.
Londay, Mrs. Isabella, 30.
London, England, 3, 5, 34.
Long, Robert, 23.
Long, Sarah Maria, 26.
Longacre, 34.
Longworth, Joseph, 63.
Lopre, Mrs. Bridget, 25.
Loudoun, Countess of, 13.
Love, Elizabeth Catherine, 47.
Lovell, Josiah Sturgis, 36.
Lowe, Margaret, 30.
Luscomb, Mrs. Elizabeth, 26.
Luscombe, Mrs. Dorothea M., 31.
Lusher, George, 28.
Maccho, Clarissa, 23.
Mackay, James, 55.
Mackay, Dr. John, 47.
Mackay, Sarah M., 47.
Macleod, Hannah, 29.
Macnamara, John, 55.
Magazine, 5 (3).
Magnier, James, 29.
Maine, Elizabeth, 44.
Maine, James, 44.
Mair, James, 17.
Malcolmson, Rev. Mr., 11 (2), 12.
Mallison, Mrs. Sarah, 15.
Malton, England, 17.
Man, Spencer John, 49.
Manchester, 59.
Manigault, Elizabeth, 49.
Manson, Elizabeth, 27.
Marchant, Peter Timothy, 4.
Marchant, Willington & Co., 4, 5 (2).
Marion, Francis, Jr., 40.
Markley, Abraham, 7.
Markley, Elizabeth, 7.
Marks, Mark, 60.
Marley, Peter, 31.
Marseilles, 58.
Marsh, Ann Louisa, 50.
Marsh, Rev. Samuel, 36, 49.
Marshall, John, 47.
Marshall, Mrs. Mary G., 43.
Martin, Ann Catherine, 60.
Martin, Catherine, 38.
Martin, Charles, Jr., 36.
Martin, Eliza, 59.
Martin, Elizabeth P., 35.
Martin, Dr. James, 35 (2).
Martin, John C., 55.
Martin, John Nicholas, 18.
Martin, Mary, 35.
Maryland, 56.
Massachusetts, 3 (2).
Master in Equity, Charleston District, 54.
Mathewes, Ann, 54.
Mathewes, Rev. Edmund, 34.
Mathewes, John R., 33.
Mathewes, William, 54.
Mathews, Rev. Philip, 17, 18, 23, 36, 44.
Mathews, Thomas, 27.
Matthisen, C. F., 58.
Maull, James, 12.
Maxcy, Rev. Jonathan, D. D., 38 (2), 59.
Maxwell, Peter, 33.
Maxwell, Robert, 14.
May, Rose-Ann, 20.
Mayberry, Caroline, 51.
Mazÿck, Nathaniel Broughton, 6.
Mazÿck, Stephen, Jr., 62.
McCaa, John, 40.
McCall, Catherine, 38 (Kitty).
McCalla, Rev. Daniel, D. D., 7, 26, 28, 31, 57, 64.
McCliesh, James, 59.
McCliesh, Jane, 53.
McClusken, Mary Ann, 9.
McCord's Ferry, 22.
McCulloch, Rev. Matthew, 15, 16 (McCuller), 29 (McCullers).
McDonald, Mary, 63.
McDowell, William, 26.
McFie, John, 58.
McGolrita, Felix, 33.
McIlhenny, Rev. James, 22.

McKensie, Catherine, 33.
McKensie, Henry, 56.
McKenzie, John, 57.
McKey, Sarah, 24.
McKinney, Eliza, 30.
McKnight, Rev. John, 50.
McKnight, Mary, 50.
McLean, Margaret, 27.
McLeod, Rev. Donald, 17 (2), 18, 42.
McLeod, Normand, 8.
McMahan, Daniel, 18.
McMillan, Thomas, 39.
McNellage, Sarah Joyce, 56.
McNish, John, 24.
McNish, Mary, 41.
McPherson, Elizabeth M., 45.
McQuain, Rev. Mr., 58.
McWhir, Rev. William, 19.
Means, Robert, 23.
Medcalf, Maria, 47.
Medowes, George, 7.
Mege, Francis, 12.
Mege, Mrs. Rebecca, 12.
Mellard, Rev. James H., 18.
Melrose, Thomas, 54.
Mercantile Daily Advertiser, The Courier and, 5.
Meredith, E., 61.
Merger, Harriet K., 37.
Middlesex, England, 43.
Middleton, Elizabeth, 39.
Mikell, John, 14.
Miles, Eliza Smith, 33.
Miles, James, 33.
Miles, John, 56.
Miles, Robert, 33.
Miller, Catherine, 40.
Miller, Matthew, 20.
Miller, John B., 59.
Miller, John Michael, 53.
Miller, Sarah, 21.
Miller, William, 32.
Milligan, William, 33.
Mills, Honoria, 11.
Mills, Sarah, 28.
Mills, Rev. Thomas, D. D., 8, 13, 28. 33 (2), 34, 43, 54.
Mills, Thomas, 23.
Mims, Mary, 35.
Minis, Isaac, 9.
Minott, Ann, 30.
Minott, Sarah, 15.
Miot, Martha, 42.
Miot, Mary Ann, 18.
Mis-Campbell, James, 16.
Mis-Campbell, Mary, 16.
Mitchell, Agnes, 26.
Modeste, Andrew, 37.
Moira, Earl of, 13.
Moise, Aaron, 20, 52.
Moise, Hyam, 52.
Moles, James C., 63.
Money, Miss, 39.
Money, William, 39.
Monk, James, 19.
Montgomery, Rev. Benjamin R., 21, 55.
Monthly Register and Review of the United States, The, 5.
Moore, Elcey, 10.
Moore, Frances, 42.
Moore, Henrietta, 36.
Moore, James, 4.
Moore, Mrs. M., 47.
Moore, Roger, 4.
Moore, Sarah I., 59.
Morgan, Clarence, 24.
Morris, Lewis, Jr., 49.
Morriss, Mrs. Ann, 33.
Morton, Elizabeth, 34.
Morton, Sarah, 21.
Moser, Eliza, 30.
Moses, Josiah, 51.
Moss, Catharine, 36.
Mosse, Dr. George, 59.
Mosse, Sarah, 59.
Motte, A., 36.
Motte, Mrs. Eliza T., 58.
Mount Pleasant Farm, 59.
Mouzon, Samuel R., 11.
Muir, Charles, 41.
Mulin, Mrs. Maria, 52.
Mulligan, Joseph, 15.
Mullin, Matthew, 32.
Mumford, Julia Ann, 55.
Munds, Rev. Israel, D. D., 11 (4), 12, 13, 14, 15 (2), 16 (2), 19, 20 (3),

21 (3), 22, 23 (2), 24 (5), 25 (2), 26 (2), 27, 28, 29 (2), 30 (2), 31 (3),, 32, 36 (2), 38, 39, 40, 41, 43, 45, 48, 55, 60, 62.
Munro, Margaret, 55.
Murden, Jeremiah, 63.
Murdoch, Elizabeth, 15.
Mure, Flora, 13.
Murphy, Harriet, 56.
Murrell, James W., 46.
Murrell, Mary E., 59.
Murrill, Mrs. Sarah, 17.
Mushett, John, 44.
Myers, Jacob, 38.
Nail, Casper, 37.
Nail, Mary, 37.
Nankivel, Rev. Mr., 54.
Naser, Frederick, 51.
Nassau, N. P., 21.
Nauman, Ann, 55.
Neal, Daniel, Jr., 37.
Negro, 25.
Nelson, Mrs. Martha, 56.
Nervis, John, 33.
Neufville, Eliza, 45.
New Jersey, 46.
New River (a neighborhood in Beaufort District), 41, 63.
New York, 3, 5, 8, 9, 13, 17, 39 (2), 45, 46, 49 (2), 50, 57, 63.
Newbern, N. C., 39.
Newberry District, 13, 16, 35, 42.
Newman, Charles, 47.
Newport, R. I., 22, 33, 38, 40 (2).
Newspaper Press of Charleston, The, 5.
Newton, William, 30.
Nibbs, William, 35.
Nichols, Eliza, 21.
Nichols, Julius, 21.
Niderburgh, Dr. S. N., 20.
Nisbet, John, 64.
Nixon, Rev. Mr., 22.
Noble, Elizabeth, 13.
Norris, Joseph, 45.
North, John L., 29.
North Carolina, 22, 33, 36, 38, 39, 58
Northampton County, N. C., 58.
Norton, Robert G., 59.
Norton, William W., 12.
Nubey, Jane, 9.
O'Driscoll, Cornelius, 53.
O'Farrell, Rev. Dr., 16, 27 (2), 35, 58, 62.
O'Hara, Henry, 44.
O'Hear, Eliza, 6.
O'Hear, James, 6.
Ogier, Lewis, 34.
Ogier, Susan, 34.
Ogier, Thomas, 13.
Ohring, Magness, 32.
Oliphant, Dr. David, 22.
Orangeburgh, 27 (2), 35, 47, 58 (3), 62; The spelling of , 27, note.
Orr, Alexander M., 43.
Osborn, Elizabeth, 54
Osborn, Thomas, 54.
Oswald, Dr. John, 15.
Ottolengui, Esther, 61.
Overland Journey to India, 5.
Owens, James, 57.
Palmer, Rev. Benjamin M., 12, 23, 47, 56.
Palmer, John, 27.
Paris, France, 51.
Parker, Thomas, 37.
Parks, Samuel, 21.
Parsons, Joseph, 44.
Peace, Rebecca, 46.
Paterson, Ann, 51.
Paterson, Robert, 7.
Patterson, Elizabeth, 10.
Patterson, Samuel, 46.
Patterson, William, 10.
Pawley, Anthony, 52.
Pawley, Mary Man, 52.
Payne, William R., 62.
Peden, William, 56.
Peedee (describes any place on the Peedee River), 21.
Peigné, Susannah, 62.
Peirce, Maria, 40.
Pellesser, Margaretta Sophia, 39.
Pendleton, 21.
Pennall, James, 20.
Pepper, Mary W., 30.
Percy, Rev. Dr., 42, 47, 61.
Perhault, Joseph, 46.

Perrie, Ann B., 61.
Petersburgh, Ga., 26.
Peyton, Captain, 27.
Peyton, Mrs. Violetta, 27.
Pezan, T. Laimable, 28.
Phelps, Mrs. Mary, 54.
Philadelphia, 9, 11, 12, 24, 32, 41, 53, 60.
Phillips, Mr. (of Georgetown), 44.
Phillips, Elizabeth, 31.
Phillips, Rev. John, 43, 54, 58, 59.
Phillips, Rebecca, 51.
Phillips, Susan, 45.
Pickenpack, John, 49.
Pike, Nathaniel, 16.
Pinckney, Miles Brewton, 60.
Pinckneyville, 18.
Pinkerton, David, 9.
Pinkerton, Mrs. Margaretta, 9.
Pogson, Rev. Milward, 15, 19, 29, 32, 61.
Poinsett, Hannah Frances, 36.
Poinsett, Joel, 36.
Polhill, Nathaniel, 38.
Polk, Thomas, 59.
Pollock, Mrs. Mary, 46.
Pooser, William H., 58.
Porcher, James, 48.
Porcher, Marian, 62.
Porcher, Peter, 62.
Port Royal, 33.
Porteous, Jane, 23.
Porteous, Robert, 23.
Porter, John, 32.
Portsmouth, N. C., 21.
Postell, Andrew, 33.
Postell, Benjamin, 54.
Postell, Joanna, 61.
Postell, Martha Eliza, 54.
Postell, Mary, 33.
Postell, Philip S., 62.
Postell, William, 61.
Potter, George Washington, 27.
Powell, John, 23.
Powers, Susannah, 10.
Preble, George, 54.
Pressley, John, 11.
Pressley, William, 15.
Price, Rev. Thomas H., D. D., 14, 16, 29, 30, 45, 48, 52, 56.
Prieur, Mr., 28.
Prieur, Laura, 28.
Prince, Laurence, 21.
Prince George's Parish, Winyah, 8.
Prince William's Parish, 33, 44.
Pringle, James R., 45.
Pringle, John Julius, 54.
Pringle, John Julius, Jr., 43.
Pringle, Mary Elizabeth, 54.
Prioleau, Dr. Philip G., 15.
Pritchard, Paul, Jr., 6.
Providence, R. I., 9, 41.
Purcell, Arabella, 60.
Purfield, Alicia, 43.
Querard, Henry, 39.
Query, John, 11.
Quinn, Thomas Fitzgerald, 11, 40.
Raburn, David, 56.
Radcliffe, Rachel, 55.
Raguet, Condy, 53.
Raguet, Condy &, 53.
Rambert, Rachel, 12.
Ravell, John, 19.
Ravell, Mrs. Rachel, 19.
Rawdon, Lord, 13.
Reame, Rev. Mr., 37.
Recardo, R. J., 48.
Recruiting Sergeant Inn, Halifax, England, 26.
Reddall, Jane, 29.
Reed, Samuel, 35.
Rees, Dr. L. N., 64.
Reid, Rev. Mr., 42.
Reynolds, Benjamin, 45.
Reynolds, Christopher, 37.
Reynolds, Mrs. Mary, 20.
Reynolds, Mary Y., 45.
Rhett, Col. William, 4.
Rhode Island, 9, 12, 41.
Rhodes, Dr. Nathaniel H., 29.
Rhodus, Josiah, 15.
Richards, Miss, 29.
Richardson, Mrs., 34.
Richardson, Charlotte, 51.
Richardson, David, 51.
Richardson, James, 53.
Richardson, Jane Bruse, 53.
Richardson, Maria, 21.

Richardson, Thomas, 33.
Richardsonville, 51.
Richmond Argus, 25.
Riedfield, Margaret, 34.
Riggs, Thomas G., 52.
Riley, James, 51.
Riley, Susan, 60.
Ripault, Joshua, 50.
Ritchie, Agnes, 42.
Ritchie, Alexander, 42.
Rivers, Mrs. Esther, 45.
Rivers, Frances Susannah, 14.
Rivers, Henry Starling, 45.
Rivers, John, 52.
Rivers, Joseph, 14.
Rivers, Mallory, 52.
Rivers, Martha, 25.
Rivers, Mary Allston, 14.
Rivers, Mary Stiles, 27.
Rivers, Susannah Love, 52.
Rivers, Thomas, 30.
Rivers, William, 45.
Rivers, William (another), 48.
Roach, Mrs., 28.
Roberds, Reuben, 56.
Roberts, Rev. John M., 10, 19, 37, 46, 59 (2).
Roberts, Robert, 37.
Roberts, Samuel, 44.
Robertson, George, 16.
Robinson, Mrs. Elizabeth, 20.
Robinson, Susannah Fowler, 11.
Rockwell, Mrs. Gertrude, 25.
Rodick, Thomas, 28.
Roe, Rev. Dr., 13.
Roe, Salem, 38.
Rogers, Joshua, 30.
Roper, Benjamin D., 44.
Ross, David, 11.
Roulain, Robert, 48.
Round O., 20.
Rout, Mary 53.
Rowe, Donald, 47.
Rowland, Margaret D., 16.
Ruberry, Benjamin Wilkins, 26.
Ruberry, Mrs. Eliza Rhoda (Badger), 63.
Rumney, 12.
Rumph, David, 58.
Runnymede (plantation), 54.
Rush, Joseph, 37.
Russell, Mrs. Mary, 28.
Rutherford, Mrs. Elizabeth, 47.
Rutledge, John, 4.
Rutledge, Mary, 4.
Sabb, Mrs. Ann, 47.
Salkehatchie, 42 (2).
Salley, George Elmore, 58.
Salmon, David D., 24.
Salter, Mary, 12.
Sampit (describes any place on the Sampit River), 55 (2).
Sanders, John, 6.
Sandford, Moses, 12.
Sandoz, Mrs. I. F., 58.
Santee (describes any place on the Santee River), 15, 16, 36, 37.
Santee Canal Company, 3.
Saratoga, N. Y., 39.
Sasportas, Abraham, 6.
Savage, Miss, 41.
Savannah, Ga., 9 (2), 18, 22, 24, 27, 29 (2), 32 (2), 41 (2), 46, 48, 50, 58, 59, 63 (2).
Scarborough, William, Jr., 22.
Schenckingh, Barnard, 4.
Schirer, John, 19.
Schooler, Mary Ann, 57.
Schriner, Mrs. Dorothy, 49.
Schultz, John C., 15.
Schutt, Casper C., 14.
Schutt, Susannah D., 14.
Scot, James, 53.
Scot, Mary Elizabeth, 53
Scott, Rev. Alexander, 38, 59.
Scott, George, 31.
Scott, James, of St. Andrew's Parish, 6.
Scott, James, of Campbellton, 49.
Scott, Joseph Adams, 41.
Scott, Joyse Jane, 36.
Scott, William, 25.
Scott, William (merchant), 43.
Screven County, Ga., 47.
Seabrook, Anne, 43.
Seabrook, John, 33.
Seabrook, Sarah, 33.
Sergeant, Ann Eliza, 34.

Serrett, Elizabeth, 63.
Shackelford, Elizabeth C., 28.
Shanweaver, Elizabeth, 62.
Sharp, John, 26.
Shaw, Mrs., 26.
Shaw, Alexander J. C., 63.
Shaw, Thomas William, 39.
Shecut, Dr. John L. E. W., 18.
Sheppard, Thomas, 16.
Shoulters, Abraham, 60.
Shum, Catherine Mary, 48.
Siebert, Joseph, 61.
Simmons, Catherine S., 53.
Simmons, James, 53.
Simmons, Joseph, 34.
Simmons, William Winter, 56.
Simms, Jane, 15.
Simms, William Gilmore, 11.
Simms, William Gilmore (1806-1870), son of above, 11.
Simonet, Mrs. Eugene Magniant, 30.
Simonet, Stephen, 30.
Simons, Ann, 8.
Simons, Charles D., 50.
Simons, Rev. James Dewar, 42, 45, 47 (3), 48, 49, 50, 51 (2), 52, 53, 54, 55, 56, 60, 62 (2), 63 (4).
Simons, Keating, 8.
Simons, Mary, 11.
Simons, Thomas, 8.
Simpson, John, 10.
Simpson, Dr. Preeson, 59.
Sinclair, Elizabeth, 29.
Singellton, Eliza St. John, 38.
Singleton, Harriet, 11.
Skrine, Susan Mason, 12.
Slade, Laben, 11.
Slawson, Nathaniel, 31.
Smart, John Thomas, 14.
Smith, Aaron, 47.
Smith, Andrew, 20.
Smith, Mrs. Ann, 18.
Smith, Ann Maria, 56.
Smith, Archibald, Jr., 7, 18.
Smith, Benjamin Burgh, 4 (2), 4-5.
Smith, Benjamin Burgh, & Co., 4.
Smith, Catherine Eliza, 20.
Smith, Mrs. Eleanor, 24.
Smith, Elizabeth, 8.
Smith, George, 23.
Smith, George A. Z., 49.
Smith, Rev. Isaac, 25, 49.
Smith, Jane, 34.
Smith, Livingston, 46.
Smith, Right Rev. Robert, bishop of South Carolina, 54.
Smith, Robert, son of above, 54.
Smith, Roger, 4.
Smith, Rufus, 17.
Smith, Samuel, Jr., 53.
Smith, Samuel W., 24.
Smith, Col. Thomas, 4.
Smith, Landgrave Thomas, 4.
Smith, Thomas (of Philadelphia), 24.
Smith, William (merchant, of Charleston), 50.
Smith, William Loughton, 29.
Smyth, Mrs. Caroline, 59.
Snipes, Mary Clay, 19.
Snow, Chester F. C., 63.
Solomon, Solomon, 25.
Solomons, Israel, 61.
Solomons, Miriam, 49.
South Island, 57 (2).
South Carolina College, 38.
Spann, Catharine Fox, 38.
Spann, Charles, Jr., 48.
Speissegger, John, 11.
Spencer, Catherine, 50.
St. Andrew's Parish, 6, 8, 14, 34, 36, 48, 52, 60.
St. Bartholomew's Parish, 15 (3), 20 (2), 24, 54, 55, 57 (2), 60, 62.
St. Domingo, 8, 12, 24, 28 (3), 34, 37, 38.
St. George's Parish, Dorchester, 56, 61.
St. Helena Island, 35, 36.
St. Helena's Parish, 45, 58.
St. James's Parish, Goose Creek, 12, 13, 28, 29.
St. James's Parish, Santee, 6, 26, 32.
St. John's Parish, Berkeley, 16, 24, 27, 45, 47 (2), 50, 53 (2), 62 (2); Establishment of, 47.
St. John's Parish, Colleton, Estab-

lishment of, 47.
St. Luke's Parish, 23, 61.
St. Mary's, Ga., 59 (2).
St. Michael's Church, Charleston, 18.
St. Paul's Parish, 22, 25, 60.
St. Peter's Parish, 33, 48.
St. Philip's Church, 42, 46, 63.
St. Philip's Parish, 12.
St. Stephen's Parish, 17, 27, 53, 62.
St. Thomas (Island), 50.
St. Thomas's Parish, 54, 57.
Starrat, Hannah, 59.
Stateburg, 19 (2), 46, 48, 59 (2).
Steads, Mrs. Harriet, 57.
Stent, Robert, 52.
Stevens, Mrs. Ann (Palmer), 27.
Stevens, Dr. William S., 24.
Stevenson, John G., 11.
Stewart, Daniel, 15.
Stiles, Benjamin, Jr., 11.
Stillman, Rev. Dr., 8.
Stine, Samuel, 64.
Stock, John, 36.
Stock, Dr. Thomas, 34.
Stoops, B. T., 55.
Strobel, Benjamin, 51.
Strobel, Lewis, 57.
Strobel, Martin, 59.
Stroman, Margaret, 58.
Stroman, Paul, 58.
Stuart, Mrs. Margaret, 63.
Stucco plaisterers, 15, 16.
Suares, Rev. Jacob, 44, 52 (3), 61.
Sullivan, Timothy, 31.
Sullivan's Island, 25.
Sumter, Louisa, 46.
Sumter District, 59.
Sumterville, 59.
Sunbury, Ga., 19.
Swan, Robert, 40.
Sweat, Rev. James, 43 (3), 59, 61.
Swift, Emmaan, 39.
Swindersine, Sarah, 29.
Swinton, Caroline, 24.
Swinton, James, 14.
Tait, Thomas, 13.
Talvande, Maria R., 53.
Tankersley, Eliza, 40.
Tankersley, John, 40.
Tannesley, Mrs. Ann, 25.
Tart, Elizabeth G., 37.
Taylor, Catherine, 57.
Taylor, Charles, 21.
Taylor, Joseph, 41.
Taylor, Josiah, 27.
Taylor, Magdaline Bonneau, 57.
Taylor, Samuel, 57.
Taylor, Walter, 37.
Teasdale, Eliza, 39.
Teasdale, Isaac, 34.
Teasdale, Mary Ann, 34.
Theatre, Charleston, 43.
Theus, Ann, 31.
Theus, Rebecca, 11.
Theus, Major Simeon, 11.
Theus, William R., 40.
Thigpen, Rev. Mr., 41.
Thomas, George, 21.
Thomas, Maria, 21.
Thomas, Mrs. Mary, 54.
Thomas, Dr. Samuel, 7.
Thompson, Mrs. Barbara Amelia, 20
Thompson, James, 20.
Thompson, Rev. John, 9, 12, 23, 53.
Thompson, John, 26.
Thompson, Laney, 31.
Thompson, Sarah (of South Carolina), 26.
Thompson, Sarah (of New York), 49.
Thomson, Mary E., 23.
Thomson, William R., 23.
Thornton, Catharine, 19.
Thorpe Place, Middlesex, England 43.
Threadcraft, Bethel, 10.
Threadcraft, Mary Eliza, 29.
Thwaite, Joseph, 26.
Tiebout, Eliza, 22.
Times, The, 3, 12, 16.
Tingham, Clark, 21.
Todd, Elizabeth, 8.
Tomlins, James, 13.
Toney, William, 6.
Toogoodoo, 14.
Toomer, Henry B., 28.

Turner, Mary, 16.
Turner, Sterling Edward, 34.
Twiggs, Abraham, 32.
United States Artillery, 37 (2).
United States Navy, 39.
Valk, Jacob R., 22.
Van Horn, Rev. J., 39.
Vanderherchen, Eleanor F., 41.
Vardell, Thomas A., 45.
Vaux, Percival Edwards, 29.
Vaux, Sarah M., 33.
Vaux, William, 33.
Verdier, Eliza, 57.
Verdier, J. M., 57.
Veree, George, 6.
Vernon, Miss, 22.
Vernon, Henry, 55.
Vesey, Capt. Joseph, 8.
Vinson, Mrs. Elizabeth, 8.
Vinyard, John, 35.
Virginia, 16, 25 (2).
Waccamaw (describes any place on the Waccamaw River), 29, 52.
Waddel, Rev. Moses, D. D., 21, 55.
Wadmalaw Island, 6, 11, 15, 19, 33, 37, 42, 45, 57.
Wagoner, Christopher, 7.
Waldrop, Isaac, 13.
Wales, Sally, 17.
Walker, Edward, 39.
Walker, Judith, 55.
Wallis, Margaret, 60.
Walnut Hill (plantation), 58.
Walter, Jacob, 15.
Walter, Keziah, 15.
Walter, John C., 57.
Walthamshire, Essex, England, 39.
Walton, John, 39.
Walton, William, 43.
Waring, Morton, 62.
Waring, Susan, 62.
Warren, John, 30.
Washington, William, Jr., 51.
Weatherly, Isaac, 12.
Webb, Burges, 57.
Webb, Daniel C., 27.
Weissinger, Ann Margaret, 63.
Welch, Margaret, 12.
Welch, Nathaniel G., 8.
Wells, Mrs. Hannah, 54.
Welsman, James, 52.
Weston, John Webb, 17.
Weston, William, 37.
Whaley, Mrs. Elizabeth, 33.
Wharton, Rev. Charles H., D. D., 46.
Whin Hall, Scotland, 64.
White, Right Rev. Bishop, 53.
White, Charlotte Hodgson, 47.
White, George K., 14.
White, John B., 20.
White Hall, John's Island, 27.
Whitesides, Thomas, 25.
Whiting, John, 35.
Whitney, Archibald, 50.
Wilcox, Mrs. Patience, 33.
Wilkerson, Rachel, 37.
Wilkins, Rev. Mr., 49.
Wilkins, John, 23.
Wilkins, Maria, 23.
Wilkinson, Joseph, 14.
Wilkinson, Mary, 28.
Wilkinson, Sarah D., 14.
Williams, Fanny, 38.
Williams, Simmson, 51.
Williamson, Thomas, 27.
Willingham, Mrs. Deborah, 9.
Willington, A. S., 3 (2), 4 (2).
Willis, Jane, 35.
Willis, John H., 60.
Willis, Mrs. Mary, 41.
Wilmington, N. C., 22, 33, 36, 38
Wilson, Barbara, 64.
Wilson, Hugh, Jr., 17.
Wilson, John, 64.
Wilson, Mary, 54.
Wilson, Dr. Robert, 54.
Wily, Elizabeth, 39.
Wingate, Edward, 22.
Winnsborough, 42.
Withers, Ann Eliza, 49.
Withers, John, 13.
Withers, Capt. John, 49.
Withers, John, Jr., 12.
Withers, Rebecca, 13.
Withers, Sophia Jane, 36.
Witter, Eliza, 46.
Wolfe, Ann, 24.
Wood, Martha, 43.

Wood, R., 17.
Wood, Rebecca, 52.
Woodcraft, Martha, 44.
Woodell, Mrs. Susannah, 35.
Woodward, Elisha, 44.
Woodward, John Hancock, 60.
Woolf, Cecilia, 52.
Woolf, Solomon, 52.
Wragg, Charlotte, 29.
Wragg, Henrietta, 19.
Wragg, William, 19, 29.
Wrexham, Denbyshire, England, 61.
Wyant, Mrs. C., 13.
Wyatt, Peter, 27.
Yates, Mary Ann, 36.
Yates, Sarah, 10.
Yates, Sarah C., 31.
Yeomans, Rev. John, 56, 57.
Yonge, Eliza, 13.
Yongue, Elizabeth P., 42.
Yongue, Rev. Samuel W., 42.
York (England) *Herald*, 17.
Young, James, 25.
Young, Mary, 38.
Young, Sarah, 39.
"Youngschool, W. F.", 5.
Zuill, William, 9.
Zylstra, John, 48.